KU-488-428

THE ALL-COLOUR COOKBOOK

THE ALL-COLOUR COOKBOOK

Edited by Eileen Turner

OCTOPUS

Contents

1	Appetizers	6
2	Soups	14
3	Salads	22
4	Vegetables	28
5	Eggs & egg dishes	36
6	Rice, pasta & pizzas	42
7	Fish	52
8	Meat	62
9	Poultry & game	90
10	Dishes without meat	104
11	Light meals, picnics & barbecues	110
12	Desserts	122
13	Baking	136
14	Drinks	154
15	Basic recipes	160
	Index	166

First published 1976 by Octopus
Books Limited, 59 Grosvenor Street,
London W1

Reprinted 1977

© 1976 Octopus Books Ltd.

ISBN 7064 0537 4

Printed in Czechoslovakia
by Svoboda, Prague
50343

Appetizers

Avocado surprise with tuna fish and cream cheese

METRIC/IMPERIAL
1 avocado pear
30 ml./2 tablespoons tuna
  fish, drained of oil
30 ml./2 tablespoons cream
  cheese
15 ml./1 tablespoon lemon
  juice
shake of pepper
black olives to garnish

AMERICAN
1 avocado
2 tablespoons tuna fish,
  drained of oil
2 tablespoons cream cheese
1 tablespoon lemon juice
shake of pepper
black olives to garnish

Cut the avocado in half and remove the stone. Scoop out some of the flesh and place it in a small bowl. Add the other ingredients and beat well. Pile the mixture into the avocado halves and garnish with an olive. *Serves 2*

Avocado surprise with tuna fish and cream cheese

Avocado cream dip

METRIC/IMPERIAL	AMERICAN
2 avocado pears	2 avocados
30 ml./2 tablespoons lemon juice	2 tablespoons lemon juice
45 ml./3 tablespoons mayonnaise	3 tablespoons mayonnaise
1 very small onion, or 2–3 spring onions, finely chopped	1 very small onion, or 2–3 scallions, finely chopped
30 ml./2 tablespoons soured cream	2 tablespoons soured cream
30 ml./2 tablespoons double cream	2 tablespoons heavy cream
salt and pepper	salt and pepper
shelled prawns to garnish	shelled shrimp to garnish

Halve the avocados and remove the stones. Spoon the flesh into a bowl, taking care not to damage the skins. Reserve the skins. Add the lemon juice and mash thoroughly. Blend in all the other ingredients except the prawns (shrimp). Pile the mixture in the skins and top with the prawns (shrimp). *Serves 4*

Melon and pineapple dip

METRIC/IMPERIAL	AMERICAN
1 Charentais or large Ogen melon	1 Canteloup melon
½ kg./1 lb. cream cheese	2 cups cream cheese
150 ml./5 fl. oz. natural yoghurt	⅝ cup natural yoghurt
15 ml./1 tablespoon tomato purée	1 tablespoon tomato purée
1 can pineapple pieces, drained	1 can pineapple pieces, drained
30 ml./2 tablespoons chopped parsley	2 tablespoons chopped parsley
salt and pepper	salt and pepper

Cut the top off the melon and scoop out the pulp from the piece removed. Remove the seeds and scoop the pulp from the melon; use a scoop to make a few melon balls for the garnish.

Blend the cream cheese, yoghurt and tomato purée until smooth. Stir in the melon pulp, pineapple pieces and parsley. Mix thoroughly, adding a little of the pineapple syrup if the mixture is too stiff. Season well. Spoon the mixture into the melon case and top with the melon balls. *Serves 8*

Left : Melon and pineapple dip
Centre : Kipper and grapefruit dip

Kipper and grapefruit dip

METRIC/IMPERIAL	AMERICAN
2 rashers lean bacon	2 slices lean bacon
2 fairly large grapefruit	2 fairly large grapefruit
350 g./12 oz. cottage cheese	1½ cups cottage cheese
1 small onion, chopped	1 small onion, chopped
90 ml./6 tablespoons double cream	½ cup heavy cream
30 ml./2 tablespoons chopped parsley	2 tablespoons chopped parsley
1 can kipper fillets, drained and flaked	1 can kipper fillets, drained and flaked
salt and pepper	salt and pepper

Fry or grill (broil) the bacon until crisp. Reserve four pieces for the garnish and chop the rest finely. Halve the grapefruit and scoop out the pulp; reserve the skins. Press the pulp through a strainer to extract the juice. Mix the juice with the cottage cheese, chopped bacon, onion and cream. Blend thoroughly, then add the parsley and the kipper fillets; reserve four pieces of kipper for the garnish. Season the mixture well and pile into the grapefruit cases. Garnish with the bacon and kipper. *Serves 4*

Top : Mushroom rice salad ; Centre : Vegetable salad Niçoise ; Bottom left : Orange herring salad ; Bottom right : Bean and salami salad

Four simple hors d'oeuvre

Bean and salami salad
Rub the salad bowl with a cut garlic clove. Mix diced salami and cooked broad beans (fava or lima beans). Toss in oil and vinegar and season well.
To vary, diced frankfurters, ham or garlic sausage may be used instead of salami.

Orange herring salad
Mix segments of fresh orange with soused or rollmop herrings. Season well. Arrange on a bed of lettuce.
To vary, use portions of smoked trout or smoked mackerel with orange or other fairly sharp fruit. Serve with horseradish cream.

Vegetable salad Niçoise
Mix sliced or quartered tomatoes, tiny cooked whole or sliced new potatoes, diced cooked green beans and black olives. Toss in oil and vinegar and season well.

Mushroom rice salad
Cook long grain rice in boiling salted water until just tender. Drain and toss in well-seasoned oil and vinegar. Allow to cool, then mix with strips of green pepper, sliced raw button mushrooms and sultanas (golden raisins).
To vary, add chopped anchovy fillets; or add pine nuts or blanched almonds; or mix with cooked peas, flaked salmon and diced cucumber.

Raw mushroom salad

METRIC/IMPERIAL	AMERICAN
350 g./12 oz. button mushrooms	3¼ cups button mushrooms
1 garlic clove	1 garlic clove
2.5 ml./½ teaspoon finely grated lemon rind	½ teaspoon finely grated lemon rind
45 ml./3 tablespoons olive oil	3 tablespoons olive oil
45 ml./ 3 tablespoons lemon juice	3 tablespoons lemon juice
pinch of grated nutmeg	pinch of grated nutmeg
salt and pepper to taste	salt and pepper to taste
4 anchovy fillets, or parsley, to serve	4 anchovy fillets, or parsley, to serve

Wipe the mushrooms clean and cut them into thin slices. Cut the garlic clove in half and rub it round the inside of a wooden or glass salad bowl. Add the lemon rind, oil, lemon juice, nutmeg and salt and pepper to taste. Beat thoroughly to mix. Add the mushrooms and toss gently with a spoon until all the slices are coated with the dressing. Cover and leave to stand at room temperature for 15 minutes.
Serve on individual plates and sprinkle with thin slivers of anchovy or with chopped parsley. *Serves 4*

Cauliflower salad

METRIC/IMPERIAL	AMERICAN
1 medium cauliflower	1 medium cauliflower
8 anchovy fillets, finely chopped	8 anchovy fillets, finely chopped
18 ripe black olives, stoned and halved	18 ripe black olives, pitted and halved
1 small onion, grated	1 small onion, grated
15 ml./1 tablespoon capers	1 tablespoon capers
90 ml./6 tablespoons olive oil	6 tablespoons olive oil
30 ml./2 tablespoons lemon juice	2 tablespoons lemon juice
15 ml./1 tablespoon wine vinegar	1 tablespoon wine vinegar
freshly ground pepper to taste	freshly ground pepper to taste

Cauliflower salad

Above : Raw mushroom salad
Right : Parma ham with melon
Below right : Asparagus on artichoke hearts

Break the cauliflower into florets and cook in boiling, salted water for 5 minutes. Drain and transfer to a bowl. Cool to lukewarm, then refrigerate for at least 1 hour.

Mix all the remaining ingredients in a bowl. Add the chilled cauliflower and toss thoroughly. Chill for 30 minutes before serving. *Serves 4 to 6*

Parma ham with melon

METRIC/IMPERIAL	AMERICAN
1 melon, chilled	1 melon, chilled
6 slices of Parma ham	6 slices of Parma ham

Cut the melon into six slices and remove the seeds. Place melon slices on a serving dish and arrange two slices of Parma ham over each one. Alternatively, cut the melon into large cubes (without the skin) and wrap a piece of Parma ham round each cube. Secure with cocktail sticks and serve on a platter. *Serves 6*

Asparagus on artichoke hearts

METRIC/IMPERIAL	AMERICAN
4 artichoke hearts	4 artichoke hearts
1 kg./2 lb. asparagus	2 lb. asparagus
4 eggs, hardboiled	4 eggs, hardcooked
hollandaise sauce	hollandaise sauce

Poach the artichoke hearts, then leave them to cool. Wash and scrape the asparagus and discard the tough part of the stalks. Tie in bundles and cook in boiling, unsalted water for 15 to 20 minutes.

Chop the eggs, mix with some of the asparagus tips and place on the artichoke hearts. Place the remaining asparagus tips on top and pour over the hollandaise sauce. *Serves 4*

Right : Speedy spiced pâté
Below left : Artichoke vinaigrette
Below right : Frosted tomato cocktail
Opposite top : Melon balls with
lemon sauce
Opposite bottom : Stuffed peaches

Artichokes vinaigrette

METRIC/IMPERIAL
4 globe artichokes
salt
French dressing

AMERICAN
4 globe artichokes
salt
French dressing

Wash the artichokes in cold salted water. Cut away any stalk and pull off any tough outer leaves. The leaves may be cut in a straight line with scissors, if wished.

Cook the artichokes in boiling, salted water until tender. Small, very young artichokes take about 25 minutes, very large ones take about 40 minutes. When a leaf can be pulled away easily, they are done. Allow to cool, then remove the centre choke.

Serve the dressing separately or spoon it into the centre of each artichoke. To eat artichokes, pull away each leaf, dip the base in the dressing and eat the tender part. The base of the artichoke, often called the heart, is eaten with a knife and fork.

Serves 4

Frosted tomato cocktail

METRIC/IMPERIAL
1 kg./2 lb. ripe tomatoes
60 ml./4 tablespoons water
salt and pepper
good pinch of sugar
little lemon juice
Worcestershire sauce to
taste
mint to garnish

AMERICAN
2 lb. ripe tomatoes
4 tablespoons water
salt and pepper
good pinch of sugar
little lemon juice
Worcestershire sauce to
taste
mint to garnish

Chop the tomatoes and put them in a pan with the water, seasoning and sugar. Heat for a few minutes only to extract the juice from the tomatoes. Rub the tomatoes through a sieve and add lemon juice, Worcestershire sauce and any extra seasoning required (e.g. celery salt, cayenne pepper or chilli sauce). Put into a freezing tray and freeze lightly.

Chop the frozen mixture lightly and spoon into chilled glasses. Garnish with mint.

Serves 4 to 6

Speedy spiced pâté

METRIC/IMPERIAL	AMERICAN
225 g./ 8 oz. liverwurst	8 oz. liverwurst
100 g./4 oz. cream cheese	4 oz. cream cheese
30 ml./2 tablespoons mayonnaise	2 tablespoons mayonnaise
45 ml./3 tablespoons double cream	3 tablespoons heavy cream
5 ml./ 1 teaspoon Worcestershire sauce	1 teaspoon Worcestershire sauce
2.5 ml./½ teaspoon curry powder	½ teaspoon curry powder
5 ml./1 teaspoon brandy or dry vermouth	1 teaspoon brandy or dry vermouth
salt and pepper to taste	salt and pepper to taste

Mix all the ingredients until smoothly combined. Place in a pâté mould lined with aluminium foil, or in individual pots, cover with clear plastic wrap or aluminium foil and chill until required.

Serve with hot toast and butter. *Serves 6 to 8*

Melon balls with lemon sauce

METRIC/IMPERIAL	AMERICAN
1 melon	1 melon
2 lemons	2 lemons
little water	little water
15–30 ml./1–2 tablespoons sugar	1–2 tablespoons sugar
To garnish	**To garnish**
mint sprigs	mint sprigs
lemon twists	lemon twists

Halve the melon and remove the seeds. Make melon balls with a vegetable scoop and chill them. Keep fragments of melon left at the bottom of the fruit for the sauce.

Grate enough rind from the lemons to give 10 ml./2 teaspoons. Squeeze the juice, measure and add enough water to give 150 ml./5 fl. oz. (⅝ cup) of liquid. Simmer the rind in the liquid and sugar for about 5 minutes. Add the odd pieces of melon, then sieve or purée in a blender. Taste and add more sugar if wished. Spoon the sauce into 4 to 6 glasses and top with the melon balls. Garnish with mint and lemon. *Serves 4 to 6*

Stuffed peaches

METRIC/IMPERIAL	AMERICAN
175 g./6 oz. cream cheese	¾ cup cream cheese
30 ml./2 tablespoons sultanas, plumped in hot water	2 tablespoons golden raisins, plumped in hot water
30 ml./ 2 tablespoons chopped walnuts	2 tablespoons chopped walnuts
2 large ripe peaches, or 4 halves canned peaches	2 large ripe peaches, or 4 halves canned peaches
4 crisp lettuce leaves	4 crisp lettuce leaves

Mix the cheese, sultanas (raisins) and nuts and form into 12 small balls. If the balls are very soft, chill the mixture for a short time. Arrange each peach half on a lettuce leaf in a small bowl and place three cheese balls on each. Serve chilled. *Serves 4*

Above : Pâté maison ; Above right : Chicken liver pâté

Pâté maison

METRIC/IMPERIAL	AMERICAN
350 g./12 oz. smoked bacon joint, boned and rolled	12 oz. smoked bacon joint, boned and rolled
15 ml./1 tablespoon clear honey	1 tablespoon clear honey
10 ml./2 teaspoons soft brown sugar	2 teaspoons soft brown sugar
8 cloves	8 cloves
6 peppercorns	6 peppercorns
pinch of dried thyme	pinch of dried thyme
1 small bay leaf	1 small bay leaf
225 g./8 oz. pig's liver	8 oz. pig's liver
1 slice brown bread, crusts removed	1 slice brown bread, crusts removed
125 g./4 oz. pork sausage meat	4 oz. pork sausage meat
50 g./2 oz. lard, melted	¼ cup lard, melted
1 small garlic clove, crushed	1 small garlic clove, crushed
grated rind of ½ lemon	grated rind of ½ lemon
1 onion, chopped	1 onion, chopped
pinch of ground allspice	pinch of ground allspice
pinch of grated nutmeg	pinch of grated nutmeg
2.5 ml./½ teaspoon salt	½ teaspoon salt
pinch of pepper	pinch of pepper
1 egg	1 egg
15–30 ml./1–2 tablespoons dry sherry	1–2 tablespoons dry sherry
1 large lemon or 5 rashers of bacon	1 large lemon or 5 slices of bacon

Put the bacon joint in a pan with the honey, sugar, cloves, peppercorns, herbs and sufficient water just to cover. Cover with a lid, bring to the boil and simmer for 35 minutes. Remove the bacon from the pan and take off the rind. Mince (grind) the bacon, liver and bread finely, then blend with all the other ingredients except the whole lemon (or bacon rashers).

Slice the lemon very thinly and use it to line the base and sides of a greased round or oval ovenproof dish. Alternatively, line the dish with the bacon rashers (slices). Fill with the pâté, cover with a lid, or foil, and place it in a roasting pan half filled with hot water. Bake in a preheated warm oven (170°C/325°F or Gas Mark 3) for 2 hours. Allow to cool completely before serving.

Serve with hot toast and butter. *Serves 6*

Chicken liver pâté

METRIC/IMPERIAL	AMERICAN
225 g./8 oz. chicken livers	8 oz. chicken livers
50 g./2 oz. butter, melted	¼ cup butter, melted
1 tablespoon sherry or brandy	1 tablespoon sherry or brandy
1 garlic clove, crushed	1 garlic clove, crushed
pinch of dried thyme	pinch of dried thyme
pinch of ground mixed spice	pinch of ground mixed spice
salt	salt
freshly ground black pepper	freshly ground black pepper
extra melted butter	extra melted butter

Clean the chicken livers well, removing any membrane or tubes. Fry the livers gently in half the butter for 3 minutes; they should still be pink inside. Remove the livers and add the sherry or brandy to the pan. Take from the heat.

Mash the livers well with a wooden spoon, add the garlic, the rest of the butter, thyme, mixed spice and a little salt and pepper. Stir in the liquor from the pan and spoon the pâté into a small earthenware bowl. Pour over the extra melted butter. Chill well.

Serve with hot toast. *Serves 4*

Prawns (shrimp) in cream sauce

METRIC/IMPERIAL
350 g./12 oz. prawns,
    cooked and peeled
freshly ground black pepper
pinch of grated nutmeg
40 g./1½ oz. butter
15 ml./1 tablespoon brandy
150 ml./5 fl. oz. double
    cream
5 ml./1 teaspoon finely
    chopped parsley

AMERICAN
12 oz. shrimp, cooked and
    peeled
freshly ground black pepper
pinch of grated nutmeg
3 tablespoons butter
1 tablespoon brandy
⅝ cup heavy cream
1 teaspoon finely chopped
    parsley

To serve
boiled rice
lemon wedges

To serve
boiled rice
lemon wedges

Season the prawns (shrimp) with pepper and nutmeg. Melt the butter in a pan and fry the prawns over gentle heat for 3 minutes. Warm the brandy in a spoon, set light to it and pour it flaming over the prawns. When the flames have gone out, reduce the heat to low and cook for 2 minutes. Then increase the heat and add the cream. Cook until the cream thickens, shake the pan and stir the sauce. Stir in the parsley.

Serve hot on boiled rice, garnished with lemon wedges.

Serves 4

Above: Prawns (shrimp) in cream sauce
Below: Prawn (shrimp) and turbot salad

Prawn (shrimp) and turbot salad

METRIC/IMPERIAL
about 175 g./6 oz. turbot
salt
100 g./4 oz. shelled prawns
90 ml./6 tablespoons
    mayonnaise
little lemon juice
1 small green pepper, diced
1 small red pepper, diced
watercress or lettuce
black olives to garnish

AMERICAN
about 6 oz. turbot
salt
1 cup shelled shrimp
¾ cup mayonnaise
little lemon juice
1 small green pepper, diced
1 small red pepper, diced
watercress or lettuce
black olives to garnish

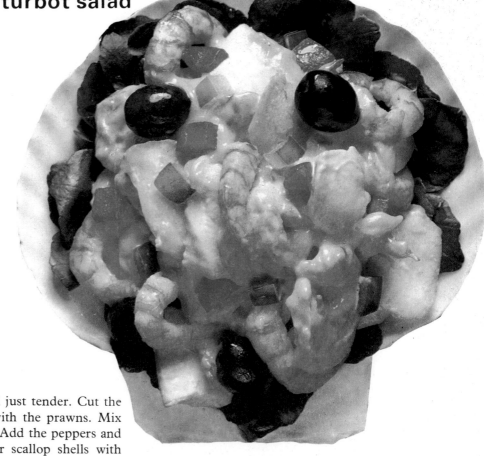

Poach the turbot in salted water until just tender. Cut the turbot into small cubes and mix it with the prawns. Mix the mayonnaise with the lemon juice. Add the peppers and the fish. Line 4 to 6 small dishes or scallop shells with watercress or lettuce. Spoon the fish mixture on top and garnish with black olives.

Serves 4 to 6

Soups

Chinese beef and vegetable soup

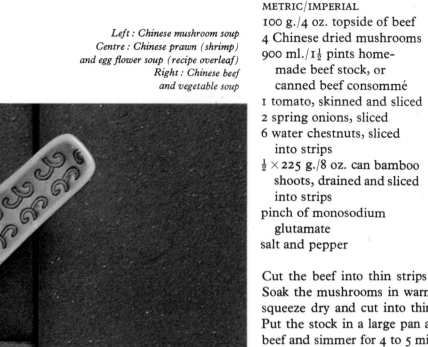

METRIC/IMPERIAL	AMERICAN
100 g./4 oz. topside of beef	4 oz. round of beef
4 Chinese dried mushrooms	4 Chinese dried mushrooms
900 ml./1½ pints home-made beef stock, or canned beef consommé	3¾ cups home-made beef stock, or canned beef consommé
1 tomato, skinned and sliced	1 tomato, skinned and sliced
2 spring onions, sliced	2 scallions, sliced
6 water chestnuts, sliced into strips	6 water chestnuts, sliced into strips
½ × 225 g./8 oz. can bamboo shoots, drained and sliced into strips	½ × 8 oz. can bamboo shoots, drained and sliced into strips
pinch of monosodium glutamate	pinch of monosodium glutamate
salt and pepper	salt and pepper

Cut the beef into thin strips across the grain of the meat. Soak the mushrooms in warm water for 20 minutes, rinse, squeeze dry and cut into thin strips, discarding the stalks. Put the stock in a large pan and bring to the boil. Add the beef and simmer for 4 to 5 minutes. Add the vegetables and cook for 2 minutes. Add the monosodium glutamate and season to taste.

Serve very hot. *Serves 4 to 6*

Left : Chinese mushroom soup
Centre : Chinese prawn (shrimp) and egg flower soup (recipe overleaf)
Right : Chinese beef and vegetable soup

Chinese mushroom soup

METRIC/IMPERIAL	AMERICAN
900 ml./1½ pints home-made chicken stock	3¾ cups home-made chicken stock
1¼ cm./½ in. slice fresh ginger	½ in. slice fresh ginger
2 spring onions, thinly sliced	2 scallions, thinly sliced
100 g./4 oz. button mushrooms, thinly sliced	2 cups button mushrooms, thinly sliced
15 ml./1 tablespoon sherry	1 tablespoon sherry
salt and pepper	salt and pepper

Put the stock in a pan with the ginger and spring onions (scallions). Bring to the boil and simmer, covered, for 20 minutes.

Add the mushrooms and simmer for 10 minutes more. Remove the ginger. Add the sherry and season to taste. Serve very hot. *Serves 4 to 6*

Chinese prawn (shrimp) and egg flower soup

METRIC/IMPERIAL	AMERICAN
2 spring onions, finely chopped	2 scallions, finely chopped
900 ml./1½ pints home-made chicken stock	3¾ cups home-made chicken stock
7.5 ml./1½ teaspoons dry sherry	1½ teaspoons dry sherry
pinch of monosodium glutamate	pinch of monosodium glutamate
pinch of sugar	pinch of sugar
5 ml./1 teaspoon soy sauce	1 teaspoon soy sauce
175 g./6 oz. peeled prawns	1½ cups peeled shrimp
1 egg, well beaten	1 egg, well beaten
salt	salt

Put the spring onions (scallions) in a large pan with the stock. Bring to the boil and simmer, covered, for 10 minutes.

Add the sherry, monosodium glutamate, sugar, soy sauce and prawns (shrimp). Reheat gently until the prawns (shrimp) are heated through. Pour in the egg and stir until it separates into shreds. Add salt to taste. Serve immediately.

Serves 4 to 6

Note: King prawns should be deveined and cut in half.

Crab bisque

METRIC/IMPERIAL	AMERICAN
1 medium cooked crab	1 medium cooked crab
400 ml./¾ pint fish stock, or water	2 cups fish stock, or water
1 lemon	1 lemon
salt and pepper	salt and pepper
bouquet garni	bouquet garni
50 g./2 oz. butter	¼ cup butter
1 onion, chopped	1 onion, chopped
50 g./2 oz. mushrooms, sliced	½ cup sliced mushrooms
275 g./½ pint single cream	1¼ cups light cream
2 egg yolks	2 egg yolks
30 ml./2 tablespoons sherry	2 tablespoons sherry

Remove all the meat from the crab, flake it and set it aside. Put the shell in a pan with the stock or water, the rind of the lemon, a little lemon juice, seasoning and the bouquet garni. Cover the pan and simmer gently for 30 minutes. Melt the butter in a large pan and cook the onion and mushrooms in it. Strain in the crab stock and add the flaked crab meat. Heat gently. Blend the cream with the egg yolks, add to the crab mixture and stir; do not boil. Add the sherry. *Serves 4 to 6*

Crab bisque

Cauliflower soup

METRIC/IMPERIAL	AMERICAN
50 g./2 oz. butter	¼ cup butter
1 large onion, chopped	1 large onion, chopped
1 garlic clove, crushed	1 garlic clove, crushed
1 medium cauliflower, in florets	1 medium cauliflower, in florets
1 l./1¾ pints chicken stock	4½ cups chicken stock
salt and pepper	salt and pepper
60 ml./4 tablespoons single cream	4 tablespoons light cream
15 ml./1 tablespoon chopped parsley to garnish	1 tablespoon chopped parsley to garnish

Melt the butter in a large pan. Add the onion and garlic and cook until soft. Add the florets of cauliflower and stock. Cover, and simmer for 1 hour.

Remove the pan from the heat and whisk well with a wire whisk or fork to break up the pieces of cauliflower. Season to taste, stir in the cream and reheat gently. Sprinkle the parsley over the soup just before serving. *Serves 4 to 6*

Right : Cauliflower soup
Below right : Chicken cream soup

Chicken cream soup

METRIC/IMPERIAL	AMERICAN
30 ml./2 tablespoons ground rice	2 tablespoons ground rice
150 ml./¼ pint milk	⅝ cup milk
1½ l./2½ pints chicken consommé	6¼ cups chicken consommé
lemon juice	lemon juice
grate of nutmeg	grate of nutmeg
salt and pepper	salt and pepper
2 eggs	2 eggs
30 ml./2 tablespoons cream	2 tablespoons cream
30 ml./2 tablespoons chopped parsley	2 tablespoons chopped parsley

Mix the ground rice with the milk until it is smooth. Heat the consommé, add the rice mixture, stir until boiling, then simmer for about 20 minutes.

Season carefully with lemon juice, nutmeg and pepper. Taste before adding salt as the consommé may be salty enough. Strain the soup and return it to the pan to heat. Beat the eggs, add a little of the hot soup, then add the egg mixture gradually to the soup. Make sure the soup does not boil. Just before serving, stir in the cream and parsley.
Serves 6

Chilled summer soup

METRIC/IMPERIAL	AMERICAN
40 g./1½ oz. butter	3 tablespoons butter
1 medium lettuce, shredded	1 medium lettuce, shredded
½ cucumber, peeled and chopped	½ cucumber, peeled and chopped
1 onion, chopped	1 onion, chopped
grated rind of 2 oranges	grated rind of 2 oranges
900 ml./1½ pints chicken stock	3¾ cups chicken stock
40 g./1½ oz. flour	⅜ cup flour
salt and pepper	salt and pepper
300 ml./½ pint single cream	1¼ cups light cream
extra diced cucumber for garnish	extra diced cucumber for garnish
quartered oranges to serve	quartered oranges to serve

Melt the butter in a large pan and add the lettuce, cucumber, onion and orange rind. Lower the heat and cook for 10 minutes. Add most of the stock. Simmer gently for 10 minutes. Mix the flour with the remaining stock and stir the mixture into the soup. Cook until the soup has thickened and season well. Purée the soup in a blender, or sieve it. Allow the soup to become really cold, then whisk in the cream. Serve chilled, topped with diced cucumber and accompanied by orange quarters. *Serves 4*

Left : Chilled summer soup
Below left : French onion soup

French onion soup

METRIC/IMPERIAL	AMERICAN
50 g./2 oz. butter	¼ cup butter
3 large strong onions, thinly sliced	3 large strong onions, thinly sliced
15 ml./1 tablespoon flour	1 tablespoon flour
900 ml./1½ pints brown stock	3¾ cups brown stock
salt and pepper	salt and pepper
For the garnish	**For the garnish**
French bread	French bread
grated cheese	grated cheese

Melt the butter in a large, heavy pan. Add the onions and cook, stirring constantly, until they are soft and golden. Stir in the flour and cook for 1 minute, then slowly stir in the stock and season to taste. Cover and simmer gently for 20 minutes.

Toast four slices of French bread and sprinkle with grated cheese. Grill until the cheese melts and bubbles. Top each bowl of soup with a slice of cheese-topped toast and serve hot. *Serves 4*

Lobster bisque

METRIC/IMPERIAL	AMERICAN
50 g./2 oz. butter	¼ cup butter
1 large carrot, finely chopped	1 large carrot, finely chopped
1 large onion, finely chopped	1 large onion, finely chopped
1 small lobster	1 small lobster
45 ml./3 tablespoons brandy	3 tablespoons brandy
300 ml./½ pint white wine	1¼ cups white wine
100 g./4 oz. rice	½ cup rice
1¾ l./3 pints fish stock	7½ cups fish stock
150 ml./5 fl. oz. single cream	⅝ cup light cream
salt	salt
cayenne pepper	cayenne pepper
parsley to garnish	parsley to garnish

Melt half the butter in a large pan and add the carrot and onion. Cook gently, stirring, for 2 to 3 minutes. Split the lobster in half lengthways, remove the coral and place the lobster, cut side down, on the vegetables. Cover the pan and cook for 2 minutes. Heat the brandy, set light to it and pour it over the lobster with the wine. Cover the pan tightly and cook very gently for 15 minutes, lightly shaking the pan occasionally. Cook the rice in 600 ml./1 pint (2½ cups) boiling fish stock for about 30 minutes, until very soft.

Shell the lobster, cut up the meat and place it in a bowl with the coral. Add the drained vegetables (reserving the liquor) and cooked rice. Pound very thoroughly to a soft pulp: this can be done in a blender, in which case add the reserved liquor. If done by hand, add the reserved liquor after the pounding is completed. Add 300 ml./½ pint (1¼ cups) fish stock and sieve.

Above : Lobster bisque

Add the remaining fish stock, pour the soup into a clean pan and reheat gently. Whisk in the remaining butter in small pieces. Add the cream and season with salt and cayenne pepper. Reheat, if necessary, without boiling. Serve hot, garnished with a small sprig of parsley. *Serves 6 to 8*

Tomato and celery soup

Below : Tomato and celery soup

METRIC/IMPERIAL	AMERICAN
25 g./1 oz. butter	2 tablespoons butter
2 medium onions, chopped	2 medium onions, chopped
3–4 celery stalks	3–4 celery stalks
½ kg./1 lb. tomatoes, skinned and chopped	1 lb. tomatoes, skinned and chopped
300 ml./½ pint chicken stock	1¼ cups chicken stock
salt and pepper	salt and pepper
15 ml./1 tablespoon concentrated tomato purée	1 tablespoon concentrated tomato purée
chopped celery leaves to garnish	chopped celery leaves to garnish

Melt the butter in a large pan and add the onions and celery; cook for a few minutes. Add the tomatoes and stock and simmer for 15 minutes. Put the soup in a blender and purée or pass it through a strainer. Return it to the pan, heat for a few minutes, then add the seasoning and tomato purée. Pour into soup cups or a tureen. Garnish with celery leaves. This soup may also be served chilled. *Serves 4*

Gazpacho

METRIC/IMPERIAL	AMERICAN
1 kg./2 lb. tomatoes, skinned	2 lb. tomatoes, skinned
½ cucumber, peeled and finely diced	½ cucumber, peeled and finely diced
1 green pepper, seeded and diced	1 green pepper, seeded and diced
1 red pepper, seeded and diced	1 red pepper, seeded and diced
6 spring onions, thinly sliced	6 scallions, thinly sliced
15 ml./1 tablespoon olive oil	1 tablespoon olive oil
15 ml./1 tablespoon wine vinegar	1 tablespoon wine vinegar
300 ml./½ pint chilled water	1¼ cups chilled water
1 garlic clove, crushed	1 garlic clove, crushed
salt	salt
freshly ground black pepper	freshly ground black pepper
sieved yolk of a hardboiled egg for garnish	sieved yolk of a hardcooked egg for garnish
ice cubes	ice cubes

Purée the tomatoes in a blender, or press through a strainer with a wooden spoon. Stir the prepared vegetables into the tomato purée with the olive oil, vinegar and chilled water. Add the crushed garlic and season to taste with salt and pepper. Chill well. Serve the cold soup in chilled soup bowls. Sprinkle sieved egg yolk in the centre of each portion and add an ice cube just before serving. *Serves 6*

Above : Gazpacho
Left : Chicken chowder

Chicken chowder

METRIC/IMPERIAL	AMERICAN
2–3 bacon rashers	2–3 bacon slices
1 onion, chopped	1 onion, chopped
400 ml./15 fl. oz. chicken stock	2 cups chicken stock
350 g./12 oz. root vegetables, diced	1½ cups diced root vegetables
300 ml./½ pint milk	1¼ cups milk
175 g./6 oz. cooked chicken, diced	1 cup diced cooked chicken
60 ml./4 tablespoons sweetcorn	4 tablespoons sweetcorn
salt and pepper	salt and pepper
chopped parsley	chopped parsley
paprika	paprika

Fry the bacon for a few minutes, then add the onion and cook together until the bacon is crisp. Add the stock and bring to the boil. Add the vegetables and cook until they are just tender. Add the milk, chicken, sweetcorn and seasoning. Simmer for a few minutes, then serve the chowder garnished with parsley and paprika. *Serves 4 to 6*

Minestrone

METRIC/IMPERIAL
45 ml./3 tablespoons oil
2 onions, sliced
2 garlic cloves, crushed
2–3 bacon rashers
4 tomatoes, skinned,
  seeded and chopped
100 g./4 oz. haricot beans,
  soaked overnight in water
  and drained
1 small glass red wine
5 ml./1 teaspoon chopped
  fresh marjoram
2.5 ml./½ teaspoon chopped
  fresh thyme
2 carrots, diced
2 potatoes, diced
1 small turnip, diced
1–2 celery stalks, chopped
½ small cabbage, shredded
50 g./2 oz. macaroni or
  pasta shells
15 ml./1 tablespoon
  chopped parsley
salt and pepper
grated Parmesan cheese

AMERICAN
3 tablespoons oil
2 onions, sliced
2 garlic cloves, crushed
2–3 bacon slices
4 tomatoes, skinned,
  seeded and chopped
½ cup navy beans, soaked
  overnight in water
  and drained
1 small glass red wine
1 teaspoon chopped fresh
  marjoram
½ teaspoon chopped fresh
  thyme
2 carrots, diced
2 potatoes, diced
1 small turnip, diced
1–2 celery stalks, chopped
½ small cabbage, shredded
½ cup macaroni or pasta
  shells
1 tablespoon chopped
  parsley
salt and pepper
grated Parmesan cheese

Minestrone

Heat the oil in a large pan. Add the onions, garlic and bacon and cook gently for a few minutes. Add the tomatoes, beans and wine and cook for a few minutes more. Then add 1¾ l./3 pints (7½ cups) water, the marjoram and thyme, bring to the boil, cover the pan and simmer for about 2 hours or until the beans are tender.

Add the carrots and cook for about 10 minutes, then add the potatoes and turnips. Cook for a few more minutes, then add the celery, cabbage and pasta. Cook until the pasta and all the vegetables are tender, then add the parsley and season to taste. Stir in 2 to 3 tablespoons grated Parmesan. Serve with extra Parmesan.
Serves 6 to 8

Salads

Mixed salad

Mixed salad

METRIC/IMPERIAL
125 g./¼ lb. tomatoes,
  thinly sliced
¼ cucumber, sliced
1 green or red pepper,
  seeded and sliced
1 celery stalk, chopped
a few black olives, stoned
  and chopped
a few spring onions,
  chopped
a few gherkins, chopped
½ crisp lettuce, shredded, or
  bunch of watercress
sour cream dressing

AMERICAN
¼ lb. tomatoes, thinly sliced
¼ cucumber, sliced
1 green or red pepper,
  seeded and sliced
1 celery stalk, chopped
a few black olives, pitted
  and chopped
a few scallions, chopped
a few dill pickles, chopped
½ crisp lettuce, shredded,
  or bunch of watercress
sour cream dressing

Arrange all the ingredients on a platter and dress with sour cream dressing just before serving. *Serves 4 to 6*

American salad

METRIC/IMPERIAL
125 g./¼ lb. green beans,
  cooked and sliced
75 g./3 oz. sweetcorn,
  cooked or canned and
  drained
½ red pepper, diced
50 g./2 oz. raw mushrooms,
  sliced
2 tomatoes, sliced
For garnish
black olives
1 small onion
French dressing

AMERICAN
1 cup cooked sliced green
  beans
½ cup cooked or canned
  and drained sweetcorn
½ red pepper, diced
½ cup sliced raw mushrooms
2 tomatoes, sliced

For garnish
black olives
1 small onion
French dressing

Mix all the ingredients in a dish and toss in French dressing. Garnish with black olives and thin slices of raw onion. Serve with cold chicken or turkey. *Serves 4*

Above: American salad;
Below: Hawaiian salad

Hawaiian salad

METRIC/IMPERIAL
1 lettuce
1–2 heads chicory
225 g./8 oz. cottage cheese
fresh or canned pineapple
    rings
2–3 oranges, peeled and
    divided into segments
1 apple, sliced
¼ cucumber, sliced
French dressing

AMERICAN
1 lettuce
1–2 heads French or
    Belgian endive
1 cup cottage cheese
fresh or canned pineapple
    rings
2–3 oranges, peeled and
    divided into segments
1 apple, sliced
¼ cucumber, sliced
French dressing

Arrange washed lettuce on a flat dish. Wash and separate chicory (endive) leaves and arrange them at each end of the dish. Spoon the cottage cheese in the centre of the lettuce and garnish with halved pineapple rings, orange segments and apple and cucumber slices, both dipped in French dressing.

Serves 4

Pasta slaw

Carrot and apple salad

Pasta slaw

METRIC/IMPERIAL	AMERICAN
100 g./4 oz. pasta rings	1 cup pasta rings
salt and pepper	salt and pepper
½ small white cabbage, shredded	½ small white cabbage, shredded
1 small green pepper, seeded and diced	1 small green pepper, seeded and diced
1 medium carrot, grated	1 medium carrot, grated
Dressing	**Dressing**
60 ml./4 tablespoons mayonnaise	4 tablespoons mayonnaise
15 ml./1 tablespoon soured cream	1 tablespoon soured cream
15 ml./1 tablespoon vinegar	1 tablespoon vinegar
10 ml./2 teaspoons sugar	2 teaspoons sugar

Cook the pasta in boiling salted water for 10–12 minutes, or until tender. Drain, rinse in cold water and drain again. Mix the ingredients for the dressing and stir in the pasta and the other ingredients. Chill well before serving.   *Serves 6*

Carrot and apple salad

Top prepared lettuce and watercress or other green salad vegetables with coarsely grated carrot, as shown in the picture. Arrange segments of apple, dipped in French dressing, as a garnish. If wished, finely chopped apple and nuts may be mixed with the carrot. Serve with cooked sausages, pork, goose or other fairly rich meats.

Chicken peach salad

Arrange prepared lettuce, watercress and chicory (French or Belgian endive) in a bowl. Top with neatly diced pieces of cold, cooked chicken, sliced fresh pear, dipped in French dressing, sliced canned peaches and fresh or dried dates. Serve with mayonnaise or French dressing and garnish with lemon.

Chicken peach salad

Tomato and orange salad

METRIC/IMPERIAL
½ kg./1 lb. tomatoes, cut
    into wedges
2 oranges, peeled and
    segmented
15 ml./1 tablespoon
    chopped fresh basil, or
    5 ml./1 teaspoon dried
    basil
finely grated rind of
    1 lemon
French dressing

AMERICAN
1 lb. tomatoes, cut into
    wedges
2 oranges, peeled and
    segmented
1 tablespoon chopped fresh
    basil, or 1 teaspoon dried
    basil
finely grated rind of
    1 lemon
French dressing

Arrange the tomatoes and orange segments in a serving dish.
Sprinkle them with basil, lemon rind and French dressing.
Chill for 30 minutes.
   Serve with cold meat, cold fish salads or barbecued meat.
Serves 4 to 6

Above : Tomato and orange salad
Right : Citrus green salad

Citrus green salad

METRIC/IMPERIAL
1 crisp lettuce, shredded
1 bunch watercress
2 grapefruit, peeled and
    divided into segments
2 oranges, peeled and
    divided into segments
French dressing

AMERICAN
1 crisp lettuce, shredded
1 bunch watercress
2 grapefruit, peeled and
    divided into segments
2 oranges, peeled and
    divided into segments
French dressing

Mix all ingredients in a salad bowl and toss gently in French
dressing. Serve immediately.
Serves 6 to 8

Burghul (cracked wheat) salad

Burghul (cracked wheat) salad

METRIC/IMPERIAL	AMERICAN
225 g./8 oz. fine burghul, soaked in water for 30 minutes	8 oz. cracked wheat, soaked in water for 30 minutes
6 spring onions, finely chopped	6 scallions, finely chopped
sea salt	sea salt
freshly ground black pepper	freshly ground black pepper
300 ml./½ pint finely chopped parsley	1¼ cups finely chopped parsley
300 ml./½ pint finely chopped fresh mint	1¼ cups finely chopped fresh mint
30 ml./2 tablespoons olive oil	2 tablespoons olive oil
30 ml./2 tablespoons lemon juice	2 tablespoons lemon juice
For the garnish	**For the garnish**
cucumber slices	cucumber slices
black olives	black olives

Drain the burghul (cracked wheat) and wrap it in a clean tea towel to squeeze out as much moisture as possible. Spread it out to dry further. Mix the burghul with the chopped spring onions (scallions), crushing them so that their juices soak into the burghul. Season with salt and pepper. Add the parsley, mint, olive oil and lemon juice and mix well. Taste, and adjust the seasoning to suit you. The salad should have a distinctive lemon taste. Garnish with cucumber slices and black olives. If wished, add some tomato slices, strips of green pepper and sprigs of parsley.   *Serves 8*

Above: Summer salad; Right: Orange and chicory salad and Celery, apple and beetroot salad

Summer salad

METRIC/IMPERIAL	AMERICAN
100 g./4 oz. short cut macaroni	1 cup short cut macaroni
salt and pepper	salt and pepper
1 medium can tuna fish, drained and flaked	1 medium can tuna fish, drained and flaked
1 apple, sliced	1 apple, sliced
25 g./1 oz. raisins	¼ cup raisins
25 g./1 oz. walnuts, chopped	¼ cup chopped walnuts
2 celery stalks, chopped	2 celery stalks, chopped
45 ml./3 tablespoons mayonnaise	3 tablespoons mayonnaise
few lettuce leaves	few lettuce leaves
chopped chives	chopped chives
lemon juice	lemon juice
celery leaves to garnish	celery leaves to garnish

Cook the macaroni in boiling salted water for 8 minutes, or until tender. Drain, rinse in cold water and drain again. Add the tuna fish. Set aside a few apple slices for garnish, then add the raisins, nuts, remaining apple, celery and mayonnaise. Season and mix well.

Line a dish with the lettuce leaves and pile the salad on top. Sprinkle with chopped chives. Garnish with the reserved apple slices, dipped in lemon juice, and celery leaves. *Serves 4*

Celery, apple and beetroot salad

METRIC/IMPERIAL	AMERICAN
4 celery stalks	4 celery stalks
1 apple	1 apple
1 medium cooked beetroot	1 medium cooked beet
1.25 ml./¼ teaspoon salt	¼ teaspoon salt
15 ml./1 tablespoon lemon juice	1 tablespoon lemon juice

Wash and chop the celery. Peel and chop the apple and beetroot. Mix with the other ingredients. *Serves 2*

Orange and chicory salad

METRIC/IMPERIAL	AMERICAN
1 orange	1 orange
1 large or 2 small chicory	1 large or 2 small French or Belgian endive
parsley sprigs	parsley sprigs
For the dressing	**For the dressing**
15 ml./1 tablespoon oil	1 tablespoon oil
2.5 ml./½ teaspoon sugar	½ teaspoon sugar
1.25 ml./¼ teaspoon salt	¼ teaspoon salt
15 ml./1 tablespoon lemon juice	1 tablespoon lemon juice

Peel the orange and remove all the pith. Cut the orange into very thin slices. Remove root and any tough outer leaves of the chicory (endive) and wash and dry the leaves. Arrange the chicory (endive) and orange slices on a shallow dish. Mix the dressing ingredients well and pour the dressing over the salad. Decorate with the parsley. *Serves 2*

Vegetables

Leeks mornay

METRIC/IMPERIAL	AMERICAN
8 leeks	8 leeks
salt and pepper	salt and pepper
25 g./1 oz. butter	2 tablespoons butter
25 g./1 oz. flour	$\frac{1}{4}$ cup flour
pinch of dry mustard	pinch of dry mustard
300 ml./$\frac{1}{2}$ pint milk, or half milk and half cooking liquid from leeks	1$\frac{1}{4}$ cups milk, or half milk and half cooking liquid from leeks
100 g./4 oz. grated cheese	1 cup grated cheese
paprika	paprika

Cook the leeks in boiling salted water for 10 to 20 minutes, or until tender. Drain and reserve 150 ml./$\frac{1}{4}$ pint ($\frac{5}{8}$ cup) of the liquid if needed for the sauce. Put the leeks on a heated serving dish and keep hot.

Melt the butter in a pan, stir in the flour and mustard and cook for 1 to 2 minutes. Gradually blend in the milk or milk and cooking liquid, stirring all the time, and bring to the boil. Turn down the heat, stir in the cheese and add seasoning. Pour the sauce over the leeks and sprinkle with paprika.

Serves 4

Mediterranean stuffed tomatoes

METRIC/IMPERIAL	AMERICAN
4 large tomatoes	4 large tomatoes
salt and pepper	salt and pepper
50 g./2 oz. fresh white breadcrumbs	$\frac{2}{3}$ cup fresh white breadcrumbs
1 medium onion, finely chopped	1 medium onion, finely chopped
1 garlic clove, crushed	1 garlic clove, crushed
50 g./2 oz. mushrooms, finely chopped	$\frac{1}{2}$ cup finely chopped mushrooms
8 blanched almonds, finely chopped	8 blanched almonds, finely chopped
15 ml./1 tablespoon chopped parsley	1 tablespoon chopped parsley
25 g./1 oz. butter	2 tablespoons butter
8 black olives to garnish	8 black olives to garnish

Cut the tomatoes in half, scoop out the middle part and reserve. Turn the tomato shells upside down to drain. Strain the seeds from the reserved tomato and blend the pulp with the breadcrumbs, onion, garlic, mushrooms, almonds, parsley and seasoning. Pile the mixture into the tomato cases. Put a small knob of butter on top of each tomato and place in an ovenproof dish. Bake in an oven preheated to moderate (180°C/350°F or Gas Mark 4) for 15 to 20 minutes, or until golden brown. Garnish each tomato with an olive before serving.

Serves 4

Opposite left : Leeks mornay
Opposite right : Mediterranean
stuffed tomatoes
Below : Stuffed aubergines
(eggplants)
Right : Potatoes with cheese

Stuffed aubergines (eggplants)

METRIC/IMPERIAL	AMERICAN
2 medium aubergines	2 medium eggplants
salt and pepper	salt and pepper
olive oil	olive oil
75 g./3 oz. fresh white breadcrumbs	1 cup fresh white breadcrumbs
2 hard-boiled eggs, chopped	2 hard-cooked eggs, chopped
8 green olives, stoned and sliced	8 green olives, pitted and sliced
1 small garlic clove, crushed	1 small garlic clove, crushed
8 anchovy fillets, chopped	8 anchovy fillets, chopped
squeeze of lemon juice	squeeze of lemon juice
15 ml./1 tablespoon chopped parsley	1 tablespoon chopped parsley
5 ml./1 teaspoon dried marjoram	1 teaspoon dried marjoram
parsley sprigs to garnish	parsley sprigs to garnish

Cut the aubergines (eggplants) in half lengthways. Make gashes in the flesh with a knife and stand them, cut side uppermost, on an oiled roasting pan. Sprinkle with salt and pepper and brush fairly thickly with olive oil. Cook in the centre of an oven preheated to moderate (180°C/350°F or Gas Mark 4) for 30 minutes. Remove from the oven and leave them to cool slightly. Carefully cut out the flesh, leaving an aubergine (eggplant) shell of 6 mm./¼ in. Chop the flesh finely and put it in a bowl. Add the remaining ingredients and season to taste, taking into account the saltiness of the anchovies. Put the mixture in the aubergine (eggplant) shells and sprinkle lightly with olive oil. Cook in the centre of the oven for 30 minutes. Serve garnished with parsley sprigs.

Serves 4

Potatoes with cheese

METRIC/IMPERIAL	AMERICAN
½ kg./1 lb. potatoes, thinly sliced	1 lb. potatoes, thinly sliced
300 ml./½ pint white stock	1¼ cups white stock
1 egg, beaten	1 egg, beaten
salt and pepper	salt and pepper
1.25 ml./¼ teaspoon grated nutmeg	¼ teaspoon grated nutmeg
50 g./2 oz. grated Gruyère cheese	½ cup grated Gruyère cheese
1 garlic clove, halved	1 garlic clove, halved
25 g./1 oz. butter	2 tablespoons butter

Put the potatoes in a bowl and add the stock with the egg beaten into it. Season with salt, pepper and nutmeg. Add the grated cheese and mix thoroughly.

Grease an ovenproof dish and rub it with the cut garlic clove. Add the potato mixture and dot with small pieces of butter. Cook in an oven preheated to warm (170°C/325°F or Gas Mark 3) for 35 to 40 minutes, or until the potato is cooked and the top is beginning to brown. *Serves 4*

French fried fennel

Ratatouille

METRIC/IMPERIAL	AMERICAN
1 medium to large aubergine, sliced and sprinkled with salt	1 medium to large eggplant, sliced and sprinkled with salt
225 g./½ lb. courgettes, sliced and sprinkled with salt	½ lb. zucchini, sliced and sprinkled with salt
60 ml./4 tablespoons olive oil	4 tablespoons olive oil
½ kg./1 lb. tomatoes, skinned	½ lb. tomatoes, skinned
2 medium onions, sliced	2 medium onions, sliced
1–2 garlic cloves, crushed	1–2 garlic cloves, crushed
1 green pepper, seeded and cut into strips	1 green pepper, seeded and cut into strips
1 red pepper, seeded and cut into strips	1 red pepper seeded and cut into strips
salt and pepper	salt and pepper
chopped parsley to garnish (optional)	chopped parsley to garnish (optional)

Leave the salted aubergine (eggplant) and courgette (zucchini) slices for about 30 minutes. Then wipe away excess moisture to remove any bitterness.

Heat the olive oil in a pan, add the tomatoes and onions and cook gently for a few minutes. Add the rest of the vegetables and stir well. Season and cover the pan with a tightly fitting lid. Simmer gently for about 30 minutes. Garnish with chopped parsley if wished. Ratatouille may be served hot or cold. *Serves 6 to 8*

French fried fennel

METRIC/IMPERIAL	AMERICAN
1 fennel root	1 fennel root
50 g./2 oz. flour	½ cup flour
salt	salt
1 egg, beaten	1 egg, beaten
90 ml./6 tablespoons milk	6 tablespoons milk
oil or fat for frying	oil or fat for frying

Wash the fennel and remove the green leaves, reserving some for garnish. Slice the fennel root and separate it into rings.

Sift the flour into a bowl with a pinch of salt. Make a well in the middle, drop in the egg and gradually mix in the flour. Beat in the milk to make a smooth batter.

Heat the oil or fat in a deep pan. Coat the fennel rings in the batter and fry for 2 to 3 minutes, until the batter is crisp. Garnish with the reserved fennel leaves. *Serves 4*

Above : Ratatouille
Right : Red cabbage (recipe overleaf)

Red cabbage

METRIC/IMPERIAL
1 medium red cabbage,
  finely shredded
½ kg./1 lb. cooking apples,
  peeled, cored and sliced
125 ml./¼ pint water
45 ml./3 tablespoons sugar
5 ml./1 teaspoon salt
4 cloves
75 ml./5 tablespoons vinegar
50 g./2 oz. butter
15 ml./1 tablespoon
  redcurrant jelly

AMERICAN
1 medium red cabbage,
  finely shredded
1 lb. cooking apples,
  peeled, cored and sliced
⅝ cup water
3 tablespoons sugar
1 teaspoon salt
4 cloves
5 tablespoons vinegar
¼ cup butter
1 tablespoon redcurrant
  jelly

Put the cabbage and apples in a saucepan with the water,
sugar, salt, cloves and vinegar. Cover and simmer for 1½–2
hours. Just before the end of the cooking time, stir in the
butter and redcurrant jelly. *Serves 4*

Red peppers

METRIC/IMPERIAL
45 ml./3 tablespoons olive
  oil
15 ml./1 tablespoon butter
1 small onion, finely
  chopped
½ garlic clove, crushed
4 red peppers, seeded and
  cut into strips
4–5 tomatoes, skinned and
  quartered
salt and pepper
chopped parsley (optional)

AMERICAN
3 tablespoons olive oil
1 tablespoon butter
1 small onion, finely
  chopped
½ garlic clove, crushed
4 red peppers, seeded and
  cut into strips
4–5 tomatoes, skinned and
  quartered
salt and pepper
chopped parsley (optional)

Heat the oil and butter in a pan, add the onion and garlic
and cook until the onion is soft and transparent. Add the
peppers and a little salt, cover and cook gently for 15 minutes.
  Add the tomatoes, cover, and cook over low heat for about
30 minutes. Chopped parsley may be sprinkled over the
dish before serving. *Serves 4*

Above: Red peppers
Right: Broccoli polonaise (top), Carrots and fried almonds (below left)
and Peas and cucumber (below right)

Broccoli polonaise

METRIC/IMPERIAL
½ kg./ 1 lb. fresh or frozen
  broccoli spears
salt
75 g./3 oz. butter
75 g./3 oz. fresh white
  breadcrumbs
2 hard-boiled eggs,
  whites finely chopped
  and yolks sieved
30 ml./2 tablespoons
  chopped parsley

AMERICAN
1 lb. fresh or frozen broccoli
  spears
salt
⅜ cup butter
1 cup fresh white
  breadcrumbs
2 hard-cooked eggs,
  whites finely chopped
  and yolks sieved
2 tablespoons chopped
  parsley

Cook the broccoli in boiling salted water for 5 minutes if
frozen and 20 minutes if fresh. Drain well, put in a heated
serving dish and add one-third of the butter. Set aside and
keep hot.
  Fry the breadcrumbs in the remaining butter until they
are crisp and golden. Sprinkle them over the broccoli.
Arrange a circle of egg white around the edge of the dish, then
a circle of egg yolk and then a circle of parsley. *Serves 4*

Peas and cucumber

METRIC/IMPERIAL
1 medium cucumber,
  peeled and diced
25 g./1 oz. butter
200 g./8 oz. frozen peas,
  or fresh podded peas
salt

AMERICAN
1 medium cucumber,
  peeled and diced
2 tablespoons butter
8 oz. frozen peas, or
  fresh hulled peas
salt

Cook the cucumber gently in the butter, stirring frequently, until it is pale golden. Meanwhile, cook the peas in boiling salted water for 5 minutes, or 15–20 minutes for fresh peas. Drain the peas and mix with the cucumber.   *Serves 4*

Carrots and fried almonds

METRIC/IMPERIAL
½ kg./1 lb. carrots, sliced
salt
50 g./2 oz. blanched
  almonds
25 g./1 oz. butter

AMERICAN
1 lb. carrots, sliced
salt
⅓ cup blanched almonds
2 tablespoons butter

Put the carrot slices in a pan with just enough salted water to cover. Cook, tightly covered, for 10–15 minutes. Meanwhile fry the almonds in the butter, stirring, until they are golden brown. Finish cooking the carrots with the lid off until all the water has cooked away. Then mix the carrots with almonds and butter.   *Serves 4*

Boston baked beans

METRIC/IMPERIAL
½ kg./1 lb. dried haricot
  beans, soaked overnight
2 large tomatoes, skinned
15–30 ml./1–2 tablespoons
  black treacle
5–10 ml./1–2 teaspoons
  made mustard
salt and pepper
350 g./12 oz. fat salt pork,
  diced
1–2 onions, thinly sliced
parsley to garnish

AMERICAN
1 lb. dried navy or lima
  beans, soaked overnight
2 large tomatoes, skinned
1–2 tablespoons molasses
1–2 teaspoons made
  mustard
salt and pepper
12 oz. fat salt pork, diced
1–2 onions, thinly sliced
parsley to garnish

Boston baked beans

Put the beans in a pan with water to cover and simmer for
10 to 15 minutes. Strain the beans but reserve 300 ml./½ pint
(1¼ cups) of the liquid. Simmer the tomatoes in this liquid
to make a sauce, then sieve it. Add treacle (molasses), mustard
and a generous amount of salt and pepper to the tomato
sauce. Put the beans, pork and onions in a deep ovenproof
dish, pour over the tomato sauce and mix well. Make sure
there is plenty of space on top for the beans to swell during
cooking.

Cover the dish tightly; if the lid does not fit well, cover
with foil before putting the lid on. Cook in the centre of
the oven preheated to cool (130–140°C/250–275°F or Gas
Mark ½–1). After 2½ hours, check the progress of the cooking.
If the beans are still hard, raise the temperature slightly.
If they are becoming a little dry, add enough boiling water to
moisten, but do not make them too wet. Continue cooking
until beans are tender, about another 3½ hours. Top with
parsley before serving. *Serves about 8*

Cheese and potato ring

METRIC/IMPERIAL
½ kg./1 lb. potatoes
3 medium onions
50 g./2 oz. butter
175 g./6 oz. cheese,
  coarsely grated
salt and pepper
paprika
parsley sprigs to garnish

AMERICAN
1 lb. potatoes
3 medium onions
¼ cup butter
1½ cups coarsely grated
  cheese
salt and pepper
paprika
parsley sprigs to garnish

Grate the potatoes and onions very coarsely or cut them into
small, thin strips. Melt the butter in a pan and toss the
vegetables in it with half the cheese and plenty of salt,
pepper and paprika. Put a well-greased ring pan (about
20 cm./8 in. in diameter) in a preheated moderate oven
(180°C/350°F or Gas Mark 4). When the tin is very hot,
remove it from the oven and press the potato mixture into
it, pressing down well. Cover with greased foil and bake
in the oven for 45 minutes. Turn out carefully on to a heated
ovenproof dish. Spoon the rest of the cheese over the ring
at intervals and return it to the oven for 5 to 10 minutes, or
until the cheese has melted. Garnish the ring with parsley
sprigs. *Serves 4 to 6*

Cauliflower with brown sauce topping

METRIC/IMPERIAL	AMERICAN
1 cauliflower	1 cauliflower
pinch of salt	pinch of salt
chopped parsley	chopped parsley
For the brown sauce	**For the brown sauce**
tomato juice (see method)	tomato juice (see method)
25 g./1 oz. butter	2 tablespoons butter
25 g./1 oz. flour	$\frac{1}{4}$ cup flour
little yeast extract	little yeast extract

Cut the cauliflower into florets and cook in about 1½ cm. (3 in.) boiling salted water for 10 to 15 minutes, or until just tender. Drain and reserve the liquid for the sauce. Keep the cauliflower hot.

To make the sauce, measure the cooking liquid and make it up to 300 ml./½ pint (1¼ cups) with tomato juice. Melt the butter in a pan, stir in the flour and cook gently for 2 minutes. Gradually stir in the liquid, bring to the boil and stir until the sauce thickens. Add enough yeast extract to give a fairly pronounced flavour. Put the cauliflower in a serving dish and pour the sauce over. Sprinkle with parsley. *Serves 4*

Right : Cauliflower with brown sauce topping
Below : Cheese and potato ring

Eggs & egg dishes

Bornholm omelet

METRIC/IMPERIAL	AMERICAN
6–8 eggs	6–8 eggs
30 ml./2 tablespoons single cream or milk	2 tablespoons light cream or milk
salt and pepper	salt and pepper
50 g./2 oz. butter	¼ cup butter
1 × 200 g./7 oz. can herring fillets, drained and cut into strips	1 × 7 oz. can herring fillets, drained and cut into strips
few radishes, sliced	few radishes, sliced
few lettuce leaves, shredded	few lettuce leaves, shredded
30 ml./2 tablespoons chopped chives or spring onions	2 tablespoons chopped chives or scallions

Beat the eggs with the cream, or milk, and seasoning. Melt the butter in a large omelet pan, pour in the eggs and cook rapidly, stirring with a fork. Bring some of the cooked mixture to the centre, allowing the uncooked egg to come into contact with the pan. When the egg is just set and the underside is a light golden brown, slide the omelet (without folding) onto a heated serving dish. Top with the herring pieces, radish slices, shredded lettuce and the chives or spring onions (scallions). *Serves 4 to 6*

Cheese soufflé

METRIC/IMPERIAL	AMERICAN
25 g./1 oz. butter	2 tablespoons butter
25 g./1 oz. flour	¼ cup flour
150 ml./¼ pint milk	⅝ cup milk
2.5 ml./½ teaspoon salt	½ teaspoon salt
pinch of cayenne pepper	pinch of cayenne pepper
1.25 ml./¼ teaspoon dry mustard	¼ teaspoon dry mustard
4 eggs, separated	4 eggs, separated
75 g./3 oz. cheese, grated	¾ cup grated cheese

Melt the butter in a large pan, stir in the flour and cook for a minute or two. Gradually blend in the milk, stirring all the time with a wooden spoon. Cook until the sauce is thick, then add the seasonings. Remove from the heat and add the egg yolks, then the cheese. Whisk the egg whites until stiff, then fold them into the mixture. Put the mixture in a greased soufflé dish and cook in the centre of an oven preheated to fairly hot (190–200°C/375–400°F or Gas Mark 5–6) for about 30 minutes. Serve immediately.

Serves 4 as a main dish or 6 as a savoury

Scotch eggs

Cheese omelet

Scotch eggs

METRIC/IMPERIAL	AMERICAN
4 eggs, hard-boiled	4 eggs, hard-cooked
little flour	little flour
salt and pepper	salt and pepper
350 g./12 oz. sausage meat	12 oz. sausage meat
1 egg, beaten	1 egg, beaten
45 ml./3 tablespoons dry breadcrumbs	3 tablespoons dry breadcrumbs
deep fat or oil for frying	deep fat or oil for frying

When the eggs are cool, coat each one in a little seasoned flour. Divide the sausage meat into four equal portions and press them out into squares on a floured board. Wrap a square of sausage meat round each egg, seal the edges and roll into a neat shape. Coat the eggs in beaten egg and crumbs. Deep fry the eggs until they are golden brown. Cool them, then cut in half to serve. *Serves 4*

Pipérade

METRIC/IMPERIAL	AMERICAN
50 g./2 oz. butter	¼ cup butter
1 green pepper and 1 red pepper, seeded and diced	1 green pepper and 1 red pepper, seeded and diced
1 small onion, finely chopped	1 small onion, finely chopped
2 tomatoes, skinned and chopped	2 tomatoes, skinned and chopped
1 garlic clove, crushed	1 garlic clove, crushed
6 eggs, beaten	6 eggs, beaten
salt and pepper	salt and pepper

Melt the butter in a heavy frying pan. Add the peppers, onion, tomatoes and garlic. Cook gently until tender, then add the seasoned beaten eggs and stir with a wooden spoon until the eggs are just set. Serve with French bread or hot buttered toast. *Serves 2 to 3 as a main dish or 6 as an appetizer*

Pipérade

Cheese omelet

METRIC/IMPERIAL	AMERICAN
2 eggs	2 eggs
15 ml./1 tablespoon water	1 tablespoon water
salt and pepper	salt and pepper
15 g./½ oz. butter	1 tablespoon butter
25 g./1 oz. cheese, grated	¼ cup grated cheese

Whisk the eggs lightly with a fork until the whites and yolks are mixed but not frothy. Stir in the water and seasoning.

Melt the butter in an omelet pan. Add the egg mixture and cook rapidly, stirring with a fork. Bring some of the cooked mixture to the centre, allowing the uncooked egg to come into contact with the pan. When the top is almost set add the grated cheese. When the cheese is melted and the underside of the omelet is a light golden brown, fold the omelet and turn it on to a heated plate. Serve immediately. *Serves 1*

Omelet cake

METRIC/IMPERIAL	AMERICAN
8 eggs	8 eggs
salt and pepper	salt and pepper
45 ml./3 tablespoons water	3 tablespoons water
50 g./2 oz. butter	¼ cup butter
For the sauce	**For the sauce**
700 g./1½ lb. tomatoes, skinned and chopped	1½ lb. tomatoes, skinned and chopped
50 g./2 oz. minced beef	2 oz. ground beef
1 garlic clove, crushed	1 garlic clove, crushed
1 onion, chopped	1 onion, chopped
salt and pepper	salt and pepper
pinch of dried or fresh basil	pinch of dried or fresh basil
Layer one	**Layer one**
100 g./4 oz. mixed cooked vegetables	1 cup mixed cooked vegetables
little butter	little butter
Layer two	**Layer two**
100 g./4 oz. mushrooms, chopped	4 oz. mushrooms, chopped
50 g./2 oz butter	¼ cup butter
Layer three	**Layer three**
100 g./4 oz. cooked prawns	1 cup cooked shrimp
little butter	little butter

First make the sauce. Simmer the tomatoes in a pan until the juice flows. Then add the beef, garlic, onion, seasoning and herbs. Simmer for about 30 minutes, then sieve if wished. Keep hot.

Heat the mixed vegetables in the minimum of butter. Cook the mushrooms in butter. Toss the prawns (shrimp) in butter.

Beat the eggs with the seasoning and water. Make four omelets, cooking each one as follows. Heat a quarter of the butter in an omelet pan and add a quarter of the egg mixture. Cook rapidly, stirring with a fork and bring the cooked mixture to the centre so that the uncooked egg comes into contact with the pan. Cook until the egg is set and bottom is a light golden brown. Put the first omelet on a hot serving dish. Cover it with the vegetable layer, then add the second omelet and the mushrooms, then the third omelet and the prawns (shrimp). Put the fourth omelet on top and spoon over some of the sauce. Serve the rest of the sauce separately.

Serves 4 to 5

Above : Omelet cake
Below : Scrambled eggs

Scrambled eggs

METRIC/IMPERIAL	AMERICAN
4 eggs	4 eggs
salt and pepper	salt and pepper
30 ml./2 tablespoons milk or single cream	2 tablespoons milk or light cream
25 g./1 oz. butter	2 tablespoons butter

Beat the eggs with seasoning and milk or cream. Melt the butter in a pan over low heat. Pour in the eggs and stir lightly with a wooden spoon until just set.

Serve with hot buttered toast. For a light meal, serve with creamed potatoes piped round the edge and sprinkle with paprika and chopped parsley. *Serves 2*

Cold cheese soufflé

Eggs au gratin

METRIC/IMPERIAL	AMERICAN
25 g./1 oz. butter	2 tablespoons butter
25 g./1 oz. flour	$\frac{1}{4}$ cup flour
300 ml./$\frac{1}{2}$ pint milk	$1\frac{1}{4}$ cups milk
salt and pepper	salt and pepper
100 g./4 oz. cheese, grated	1 cup grated cheese
4 eggs, soft or hard-boiled and shelled	4 eggs, soft or hard-cooked and shelled
Topping	**Topping**
30 ml./2 tablespoons grated cheese	2 tablespoons grated cheese
30 ml./2 tablespoons dry breadcrumbs	2 tablespoons dry breadcrumbs

Melt the butter in a pan, stir in the flour and cook for 1 minute. Gradually blend in the milk, stirring constantly, until the sauce thickens. Season well and stir in the cheese; cook gently until the cheese has melted.

Arrange the whole eggs in a flameproof dish and pour over the sauce. Sprinkle the grated cheese and breadcrumbs on top and brown under the grill (broiler) or in a hot oven.

Serves 2 as a main dish or 4 as an appetizer

Cold cheese soufflé

METRIC/IMPERIAL	AMERICAN
aspic jelly to set 400 ml./ $\frac{3}{4}$ pint	aspic jelly to set 2 cups
300 ml./$\frac{1}{2}$ pint very hot water	$1\frac{1}{4}$ cups very hot water
3 eggs, separated	3 eggs, separated
150 ml./$\frac{1}{4}$ pint double cream	$\frac{5}{8}$ cup heavy cream
150 ml./$\frac{1}{4}$ pint single cream	$\frac{5}{8}$ cup light cream
100 g./4 oz. Cheddar or Gruyère cheese, finely grated	1 cup finely grated Cheddar or Gruyère cheese
salt and pepper	salt and pepper
For the garnish	**For the garnish**
gherkins	dill pickle
tomatoes	tomatoes

Soften the aspic jelly, then dissolve it in the hot water. Whisk it into the egg yolks and continue whisking until it is well blended. Leave it to cool. Meanwhile whisk the double (heavy) cream until it holds its shape, then gradually whisk in the single (light) cream, cheese and seasoning.

When the aspic has just begun to stiffen, fold in the cream mixture. Beat the egg whites until stiff and fold them in. Spoon the mixture into a prepared soufflé dish and leave to set.

Remove the paper from the dish and garnish with gherkin (dill pickle) and tomato. *Serves 6 to 8*

Note: The quantity of aspic gives a very lightly set soufflé which is ideal, but it must be given time to set. If you do not have much time, use enough aspic to set 600 ml./1 pint (2$\frac{1}{2}$ cups).

Soufflé omelet

METRIC/IMPERIAL	AMERICAN
2 or 3 eggs	2 or 3 eggs
salt and pepper	salt and pepper
15 ml./1 tablespoon water	1 tablespoon water
25 g./1 oz. butter	2 tablespoons butter
For filling	**For filling**
50 g./2 oz. mixed cooked vegetables	$\frac{1}{2}$ cup mixed cooked vegetables
60 ml./4 tablespoons tomato sauce, or fresh tomato purée	5 tablespoons tomato sauce, or fresh tomato purée

Separate the egg yolks from the whites. Beat the yolks with seasoning and water. Whisk the egg whites until very stiff, then fold them into the yolks. Heat the grill (broiler). Mix the vegetables with the tomato sauce, or purée, and put over gentle heat. Melt the butter in an omelet pan until it is frothy. Pour the egg mixture in, let it set for a few seconds, then stir with a fork. Draw the cooked mixture to the centre of the pan and let the uncooked egg come into contact with the pan. When the omelet is half cooked, put the pan under the grill (broiler) to complete the cooking. Make a shallow cut across the middle of the omelet so that it will fold easily, then spoon on the filling. Fold the omelet and serve.

Serves 1

Opposite top : Eggs au gratin
Opposite bottom : Soufflé omelet

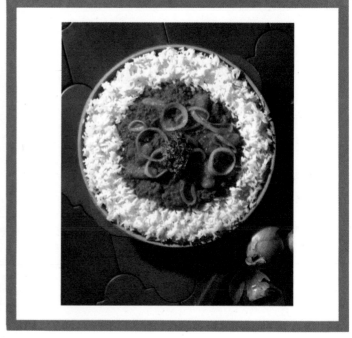

Chicken pilau

METRIC/IMPERIAL	AMERICAN
30 ml./2 tablespoons oil	2 tablespoons oil
2 onions, chopped	2 onions, chopped
1 garlic clove, crushed (optional)	1 garlic clove, crushed (optional)
225 g./8 oz. long grain rice	1¼ cups long grain rice
600 ml./1 pint chicken stock	2½ cups chicken stock
50 g./2 oz. sultanas	½ cup golden raisins
few pine nuts, or other nuts (optional)	few pine nuts, or other nuts (optional)
350 g./12 oz. diced cooked chicken	2 cups diced cooked chicken
salt and pepper	salt and pepper
few nuts to garnish	few nuts to garnish

Heat the oil in a large frying pan and cook the onions and garlic for a few minutes. Then add the rice, turning it in the oil so that all the grains are separate. Add the stock, bring to the boil and stir, then simmer in the uncovered pan for about 10 minutes. Add the rest of the ingredients and cook for 10 to 15 minutes more, until the liquid has been absorbed. Pile on to a hot serving dish and sprinkle with nuts.

Serves 4 to 5

Beef risotto milanaise

METRIC/IMPERIAL
30 ml./2 tablespoons oil
2 onions, thinly sliced
1–2 garlic cloves, thinly
  sliced
½ kg./1 lb. minced beef
1 medium can tomatoes
4 carrots, chopped
15 ml./1 tablespoon tomato
  purée
salt and pepper
1 bay leaf
225 g./8 oz. long grain rice
600 ml./1 pint water
parsley sprig to garnish

AMERICAN
2 tablespoons oil
2 onions, thinly sliced
1–2 garlic cloves, thinly
  sliced
1 lb. ground beef
1 medium can tomatoes
4 carrots, chopped
1 tablespoon tomato purée
salt and pepper
1 bay leaf
1¼ cups long grain rice
2½ cups water
parsley sprig to garnish

Heat the oil in a large pan and cook the onions and garlic until the onions are transparent. Put a few rings of onion aside for the garnish. Add the beef to the pan, stirring well to break up any lumps. Add the tomatoes and liquid from the can, the carrots, tomato purée, seasoning and bay leaf. Cover the pan and cook gently for 45 minutes, stirring once or twice.

Put the rice and cold water in a pan with ½–1 teaspoon salt. Bring the water to the boil, stir briskly, then cover the pan. Lower the heat and cook for about 15 minutes, until the rice is tender and the liquid is absorbed. Fork the rice on to a hot dish. Spoon the beef mixture in the centre and garnish with the reserved onion rings and the sprig of parsley. *Serves 4 to 5*

Risotto

METRIC/IMPERIAL
50 g./2 oz. butter
1 onion, finely chopped
1 garlic clove, crushed
225 g./8 oz. long grain rice
60 ml./1 pint chicken stock
few strands of saffron
salt and pepper
little grated nutmeg
15 ml./1 tablespoon tomato
  purée
little grated Parmesan
  cheese
watercress sprig to garnish

AMERICAN
¼ cup butter
1 onion, finely chopped
1 garlic clove, crushed
1¼ cups long grain rice
2½ cups chicken stock
few strands of saffron
salt and pepper
little grated nutmeg
1 tablespoon tomato purée
little grated Parmesan cheese
watercress sprig to garnish

Melt the butter in a large frying pan. Add the onion and garlic and cook gently until the onion is transparent. Then add the rice and turn it in the butter until every grain is separate. Blend a little of the stock with the saffron. Add the rest of the stock to the pan with the salt, pepper, nutmeg and tomato purée. Strain the saffron-infused stock and add it to the pan. Stir well. Cook gently until the rice has absorbed the liquid, stirring occasionally. Top with the grated cheese and serves, garnished with the watercress. *Serves 4*
Variations: The risotto can be varied, or made into a main dish, by adding sliced hard-boiled egg, cooked or canned red peppers (pimientos), chicken livers cooked in butter, or prawns (shrimp).

Opposite far left : Chicken pilau
Opposite above : Beef risotto milanaise
Right : Risotto

Fried rice with ham and been sprouts

METRIC/IMPERIAL	AMERICAN
30 ml./2 tablespoons oil	2 tablespoons oil
2 spring onions, finely chopped	2 scallions, finely chopped
1 garlic clove, crushed	1 garlic clove, crushed
350 g./12 oz. rice, cooked	6 cups cooked rice
150 g./5 oz. ham, chopped	1 cup chopped ham
30 ml./2 tablespoons soy sauce	2 tablespoons soy sauce
2 eggs, beaten	2 eggs, beaten
salt and pepper	salt and pepper
225 g./8 oz. canned bean sprouts, drained	8 oz. canned bean sprouts, drained

Heat the oil in a frying pan and fry the spring onions (scallions) and garlic for 2 minutes over medium heat. Add the rice, mix well and heat through. Mix the ham with the soy sauce, add it to the rice mixture and mix well. Season the beaten eggs with salt and pepper, and pour into the rice in a thin stream, stirring constantly, until the eggs are cooked. Stir in the bean sprouts and heat through. Serve immediately.

Serves 6 to 8

Noodle ring with meat sauce

METRIC/IMPERIAL	AMERICAN
30 ml./2 tablespoons oil	2 tablespoons oil
1 onion, chopped	1 onion, chopped
1 garlic clove, crushed	1 garlic clove, crushed
225 g./$\frac{1}{2}$ lb. minced beef	$\frac{1}{2}$ lb. ground beef
15 ml./1 tablespoon tomato purée	1 tablespoon tomato purée
1 green apple, cored and chopped (optional)	1 green apple, cored and chopped (optional)
salt and pepper	salt and pepper
1.25 ml./$\frac{1}{4}$ teaspoon sugar	$\frac{1}{4}$ teaspoon sugar
1.25 ml./$\frac{1}{4}$ teaspoon dried basil	$\frac{1}{4}$ teaspoon dried basil
1 × 225 g./8 oz. can tomatoes	1 × 8 oz. can tomatoes
350 g./12 oz. noodles	12 oz. noodles
chopped parsley	chopped parsley

Heat the oil in a pan and fry the onion and garlic until the onion begins to brown. Add the meat and stir over medium heat for about 5 minutes, until the meat is browned. Add the tomato purée, apple, salt, pepper, sugar, basil and tomatoes. Cover the pan and simmer for about 40 minutes. While the sauce is cooking, cook the noodles in boiling salted water for about 12 minutes, according to the instructions on the packet. Pack the cooked noodles into a buttered ring pan and keep them hot.

When the sauce is ready, turn the noodle ring on to a hot serving dish, pile the sauce in the middle and sprinkle with chopped parsley.

Serves 4

Spaghetti with tomato and anchovy sauce

METRIC/IMPERIAL	AMERICAN
30 ml./2 tablespoons olive oil	2 tablespoons olive oil
2 garlic cloves, chopped	2 garlic cloves, chopped
8 large tomatoes, skinned and chopped	8 large tomatoes, skinned and chopped
6–8 anchovy fillets, chopped	6–8 anchovy fillets, chopped
10 ml./2 teaspoons finely chopped mint, or 15 ml./1 tablespoon chopped parsley	2 teaspoons finely chopped mint, or 1 tablespoon chopped parsley
15 ml./1 tablespoon chopped basil	1 tablespoon chopped basil
salt and pepper	salt and pepper
350 g./12 oz. spaghetti	12 oz. spaghetti
butter	butter
grated Parmesan cheese	grated Parmesan cheese

Heat the olive oil with the garlic, then add the tomatoes and anchovy fillets. Cook for 10 minutes, then add the herbs and season well. Simmer gently for a few more minutes.

While the sauce is cooking, cook the spaghetti in boiling salted water for about 12 minutes, according to instructions on the packet. Drain it and toss in butter. Pour the sauce over the top and serve with grated Parmesan cheese. *Serves 4*

Opposite left : Fried rice with ham and bean sprouts; Left : Spaghetti with tomato and anchovy sauce; Below : Noodle ring with meat sauce

Spaghetti bolognese

METRIC/IMPERIAL	AMERICAN
350 g./12 oz. spaghetti	12 oz. spaghetti
salt	salt
butter	butter
grated Parmesan cheese	grated Parmesan cheese
For the bolognese sauce	**For the bolognese sauce**
25 g./1 oz. butter	2 tablespoons butter
3 bacon rashers, chopped	3 bacon slices, chopped
1 onion, finely chopped	1 onion, finely chopped
1 carrot, chopped	1 carrot, chopped
1 celery stalk, finely chopped	1 celery stalk, finely chopped
225 g./½ lb. lean beef, minced	½ lb. lean beef, ground
100 g./4 oz. chicken livers, chopped	4 oz. chicken livers, chopped
15 ml./1 tablespoon tomato purée	1 tablespoon tomato purée
90 ml./6 tablespoons white wine	6 tablespoons white wine
300 ml./½ pint stock or water	1¼ cups stock or water
salt and pepper	salt and pepper
grated nutmeg	grated nutmeg
50 ml./2 fl. oz. cream or milk	¼ cup cream or milk

First make the sauce. Melt the butter in a pan and fry the bacon, onion, carrot and celery for about 10 minutes, or until the vegetables are soft. Add the meat; when it has browned, add the chopped chicken livers. Cook for 2–3 minutes, then add the tomato purée, wine and stock or water. Add salt and pepper to taste and a grating of nutmeg. Stir the sauce until it boils, then reduce the heat, cover and simmer for about 40 minutes, stirring occasionally. Just before serving, stir in the cream or milk and check to see if it needs more seasoning.

While the sauce is cooking, cook the spaghetti in boiling salted water for about 12 minutes, according to the instructions on the packet. Drain the spaghetti, put it on a hot serving dish and put a generous nut of butter on top. Pour the sauce over and serve immediately with grated Parmesan cheese. *Serves 4*

Above left : Spaghetti bolognese
Above centre : Spaghetti with tomato sauce and olives
Above right : Lasagne

Spaghetti with tomato sauce and olives

METRIC/IMPERIAL	AMERICAN
350 g./12 oz. spaghetti	12 oz. spaghetti
salt	salt
12–16 large black olives, stoned and halved	12–16 large black olives, pitted and halved
30 ml./2 tablespoons olive oil	2 tablespoons olive oil
butter	butter
hot tomato sauce	hot tomato sauce
grated Parmesan cheese	grated Parmesan cheese

Cook the spaghetti in boiling salted water for about 12 minutes, according to instructions on the packets. Cook the olives for 2–3 minutes in a little olive oil.

Drain the spaghetti, put it on a hot serving dish and put a generous nut of butter on top. Pour the tomato sauce over and arrange the olives on top. Serve immediately with grated Parmesan cheese.   *Serves 4*

Lasagne

METRIC/IMPERIAL	AMERICAN
175 g./6 oz. lasagne	6 oz. lasagne
bolognese sauce (see recipe for spaghetti bolognese)	bolognese sauce (see recipe for spaghetti bolognese)
grated Parmesan cheese	grated Parmesan cheese
butter	butter
For the cheese sauce	**For the cheese sauce**
50 g./2 oz. butter	¼ cup butter
45 ml./3 tablespoons flour	3 tablespoons flour
400 ml./¾ pint milk	2 cups milk
75 g./3 oz. grated Parmesan cheese	¾ cup grated Parmesan cheese
salt and pepper	salt and pepper
pinch of grated nutmeg	pinch of grated nutmeg

Cook the lasagne in boiling salted water for 10 to 15 minutes, according to instructions on the packet. Drain thoroughly and place each piece on paper towelling to absorb moisture.

To make the cheese sauce, melt the butter in a pan and stir in the flour. Cook for 2 minutes, then blend in the milk. Bring to the boil, stirring constantly, until the sauce thickens. Stir in the cheese. Season with salt and pepper and nutmeg.

Butter a deep ovenproof dish. Cover the base with bolognese sauce, then add a layer of cheese sauce followed by a layer of lasagne. Repeat the layers and top with cheese sauce. Sprinkle thickly with cheese and dot with butter. Cook for 30 minutes in the centre of the oven preheated to moderate (180°C/350°F or Gas Mark 4). Serve immediately.
Serves 4

Pizza with olives and herbs

METRIC/IMPERIAL
225 g./8 oz. quantity rich
   shortcrust pastry
45 ml./3 tablespoons olive
   oil
2 onions, finely chopped
1 garlic clove, crushed
1 large can Italian tomatoes
   (about $1\frac{1}{4}$ kg./$2\frac{1}{2}$ lb.)
30 ml./2 tablespoons tomato
   purée
10 ml./2 teaspoons dried
   oregano
10 ml./2 teaspoons chopped
   fresh basil, or 5 ml./1
   teaspoon dried basil
1 bay leaf
10 ml./2 teaspoons sugar
5 ml./1 teaspoon salt
freshly ground black pepper
fresh herbs, as available
stoned green olives

AMERICAN
2 cup quantity rich
   shortcrust pastry
3 tablespoons olive oil
2 onions, finely chopped
1 garlic clove, crushed
1 large can Italian tomatoes
   (about $2\frac{1}{2}$ lb.)
2 tablespoons tomato purée
2 teaspoons dried oregano
2 teaspoons chopped fresh
   basil, or 1 teaspoon dried
   basil
1 bay leaf
2 teaspoons sugar
1 teaspoon salt
freshly ground black pepper
fresh herbs, as available
pitted green olives

Roll out the dough and line a 20 cm./8 in. diameter flan case. Place some greaseproof (waxed) paper over the pastry and put some dry beans in it. Bake the pastry case in the oven preheated to 190°C/375°F or Gas Mark 5 for 15 minutes.

To make the filling, heat the oil in a pan and cook the onion and garlic until the onion is soft and transparent but not coloured. Add the tomatoes, coarsely chopped, with the liquid from the can. Then add the tomato purée, oregano, basil, bay leaf, sugar, salt and pepper. Bring to the boil, lower the heat and simmer gently, uncovered, for about 45 minutes, stirring occasionally. Remove the bay leaf, add more seasoning if necessary and pour the mixture into the pastry case.

Sprinkle with coarsely chopped fresh herbs and a few drops of oil. Arrange the olives on top and bake in the oven preheated to moderate (180°C/350°F or Gas Mark 4) for 10 to 15 minutes, or until the pastry is golden brown.

Serves 4 to 6

Opposite above : Pizza with olives and herbs ; Opposite below : Mexican macaroni ; Above : Tagliatelle with liver sauce

Mexican macaroni

METRIC/IMPERIAL	AMERICAN
100 g./4 oz. macaroni	4 oz. macaroni
salt	salt
8 frankfurters, chopped	8 frankfurters, chopped
100 g./4 oz. cooked fresh peas	1 cup cooked fresh peas
For the sauce	**For the sauce**
25 g./1 oz. butter	2 tablespoons butter
25 g./1 oz. flour	¼ cup flour
300 ml./½ pint milk	1¼ cups milk
100 g./4 oz. grated Cheddar cheese	1 cup grated Cheddar cheese
salt and pepper	salt and pepper
5 ml./1 teaspoon made mustard	1 teaspoon made mustard
pinch of cayenne pepper	pinch of cayenne pepper

Cook the macaroni in boiling salted water according to the instructions on the packet.

While the macaroni is cooking, make the sauce. Melt the butter in a pan, add the flour and cook for 2 minutes, stirring. Blend in the milk and bring to the boil, stirring continually. When the sauce has thickened, reduce the heat and stir in the cheese and seasonings.

Drain the macaroni and add it to the sauce. Add the frankfurters with the peas. Heat for a few minutes and serve.

Serves 4

Tagliatelle with liver sauce

METRIC/IMPERIAL	AMERICAN
225 g./½ lb. chicken livers	½ lb. chicken livers
30 ml./2 tablespoons flour	2 tablespoons flour
25 g./1 oz. butter	2 tablespoons butter
15 ml./1 tablespoon olive oil	1 tablespoon olive oil
1 small onion, finely chopped	1 small onion, finely chopped
1 garlic clove, chopped	1 garlic clove, chopped
100 g./4 oz. mushrooms, sliced	1 cup sliced mushrooms
150 ml./¼ pint chicken stock	⅝ cup chicken stock
150 ml./¼ pint dry white wine	⅝ cup dry white wine
salt and pepper	salt and pepper
350 g./12 oz. tagliatelle	12 oz. tagliatelle
butter	butter

First make the sauce. Cut the chicken livers into small pieces and coat with flour. Heat the butter and oil together in a pan. Add the onion and garlic and fry gently until pale gold. Add the liver and mushrooms. Fry more briskly for 3 to 4 minutes, stirring constantly. Add the stock and wine and season to taste. Bring to the boil, stirring, then lower the heat and cover the pan. Simmer gently for 15 minutes.

While the sauce is cooking, cook the tagliatelle in boiling salted water for about 12 minutes, according to instructions on the packet. Put the tagliatelle on a heated serving dish and put a generous knob of butter on top. Pour the sauce over and serve immediately.

Serves 4

Cannelloni

METRIC/IMPERIAL
8 pieces of wide lasagne
300 ml./½ pint cheese sauce
For the filling
1 streaky bacon rasher,
  cut into small pieces
1 small onion, chopped
225 g./8 oz. minced beef
15 ml./1 tablespoon oil
1 celery stalk, chopped
½ garlic clove, crushed
1.25 ml./¼ teaspoon dried
  mixed herbs
salt and pepper
pinch of sugar
45 ml./3 tablespoons
  tomato purée
150 ml./¼ pint water

AMERICAN
8 pieces of wide lasagne
1¼ cups cheese sauce
For the filling
1 fatty bacon slice, cut into
  small pieces
1 small onion, chopped
8 oz. ground beef
1 tablespoon oil
1 celery stalk, chopped
½ garlic clove, crushed
¼ teaspoon dried mixed
  herbs
salt and pepper
pinch of sugar
3 tablespoons tomato purée
⅝ cup water

First make the filling. Fry the bacon, onion and beef in the oil until brown, stirring frequently. Add all the remaining filling ingredients and stir well. Cover and simmer for 1 hour.

Cook the lasagne in boiling salted water for 8 to 10 minutes, or according to the instructions on the packet. When it is tender, drain, rinse and drain again. Arrange the pieces of pasta on a damp towel so that they do not stick together. Place a spoonful of the filling on each piece of lasagne and roll up. Put the lasagne rolls in a greased ovenproof dish.

Pour the cheese sauce over the rolls and cook in the oven preheated to moderate (180°C/350°F or Gas Mark 4) for 25 to 30 minutes, or until the cannelloni is heated through.

Serves 4

Semolina gnocchi

50

Semolina gnocchi

METRIC/IMPERIAL	AMERICAN
600 ml./1 pint milk	2½ cups milk
150 g./5 oz. coarse semolina	1 cup coarse semolina or farina
5 ml./1 teaspoon salt	1 teaspoon salt
shake of pepper	shake of pepper
50 g./2 oz. butter	¼ cup butter
75 g./3 oz. grated Parmesan cheese	¾ cup grated Parmesan cheese
1.25 ml./¼ teaspoon grated nutmeg	¼ teaspoon grated nutmeg
1 large egg, beaten	1 large egg, beaten
extra 25 g./1 oz. butter	extra 2 tablespoons butter

Pour the milk into a saucepan. Add the semolina (or farina), salt, pepper and butter. Stir constantly over low heat until the mixture comes to the boil and thickens. Continue to simmer until the mixture is very thick, for 5 to 7 minutes. Stir frequently to prevent the mixture sticking to the pan.

Remove from the heat and beat in 50 g./2 oz. (½ cup) cheese and the nutmeg and egg. Beat until well mixed, then turn the mixture on to a flat dish, spreading it to 6 mm./¼ in. thick. Leave in a cool place for several hours, or until firm. Cut the gnocchi into 3.75 cm./1½ in. squares or rounds with a knife or cutter dipped in cold water.

Butter a shallow ovenproof dish and fill it with layers of gnocchi squares or rounds, arranged in overlapping circles. Sprinkle with the rest of the cheese and dot with the extra butter. Reheat and brown in the top of the oven preheated to hot (220°C/425°F or Gas Mark 7) for 15 minutes. *Serves 4*

Neapolitan pizza

Neapolitan pizza

METRIC/IMPERIAL	AMERICAN
Basic pizza dough	**Basic pizza dough**
1.25 ml./¼ teaspoon sugar	¼ teaspoon sugar
150 ml./¼ pint warm water	⅝ cup warm water
5 ml./1 teaspoon dried yeast	1 teaspoon dried yeast
225 g./8 oz. flour	2 cups flour
5 ml./1 teaspoon salt	1 teaspoon salt
15 ml./1 tablespoon butter	1 tablespoon butter
For the filling	**For the filling**
olive oil	olive oil
6 medium tomatoes, skinned and sliced	6 medium tomatoes, skinned and sliced
1 garlic clove, chopped	1 garlic clove, chopped
12 anchovy fillets	12 anchovy fillets
100 g./4 oz. Mozzarella cheese, thinly sliced	4 oz. Mozzarella cheese, thinly sliced
12 large black olives, stoned	12 large black olives, pitted
oregano	oregano
pepper	pepper

To make the dough, dissolve the sugar in the warm water and sprinkle the dried yeast on top. Leave the mixture in a warm place for 10 to 15 minutes, until it is frothy. Meanwhile, sift the flour and salt into a bowl and rub in the butter. Mix to a dough with the yeast liquid, adding a little extra flour if the dough is sticky. Knead for about 10 minutes, until the dough is smooth and elastic, then put it in an oiled bowl. Cover with oiled paper and leave in a warm place to rise until the dough has doubled in size.

Turn the dough on to a floured board and knead slightly until it is smooth. Roll out into a circle 6 mm./¼ in. thick and place it on an oiled baking sheet. Brush the dough with olive oil and cover it with slices of tomato. Sprinkle with garlic, then top with anchovy fillets, cheese slices and olives. Sprinkle with oregano and pepper and bake near the top of the oven preheated to very hot (230°C/450°F or Gas Mark 8) for 25 to 30 minutes. Serve hot.

Serves 1 to 2 as a light meal, or 4 as a starter
Variations: In place of the anchovies, use 50 g./2 oz. (½ cup) chopped cooked ham or 6 to 8 slices of salami. Omit the cheese and anchovies and use 100 g./4 oz. (1 cup) sliced mushrooms (first fried in a little butter) and use sliced pimiento-stuffed green olives in place of black olives.

Above : Sole normande ; Opposite above : Sole with savoury butter ;
Opposite below : Crab with black beans

Sole normande

METRIC/IMPERIAL	AMERICAN
½ l./1 pint mussels	2½ cups mussels
300 ml./½ pint water	1¼ cups water
bouquet garni	bouquet garni
salt and pepper	salt and pepper
100 g./4 oz. prawns	1 cup prawns
few oysters	few oysters
1 onion, chopped	1 onion, chopped
150 ml./¼ pint white wine	⅝ cup white wine
8 fillets of sole	8 fillets of sole
75 g./3 oz. butter	6 tablespoons butter
50 g./2 oz. flour	½ cup flour
150 ml./¼ pint milk	⅝ cup milk
150 ml./¼ pint double cream	⅝ cup heavy cream
100 g./4 oz. button mushrooms, sliced	1 cup sliced button mushrooms

Wash the mussels; scrub them well and remove any 'beard' or weed attached to the shell. Discard any mussels which do not close when sharply tapped as this means the mussel is dead. Put the mussels in a pan with the water, bouquet garni and seasoning. Heat until the mussels open, then lift them out of the liquid. Shell the prawns and open the oysters. Put the prawn shells, the liquid from the oyster shells, the onion and wine in the mussel liquid. Simmer for 15 minutes. Strain carefully and return the liquid to the pan. Put the folded fillets of sole in the pan and simmer until just tender. Lift the sole out of the liquid and arrange on a hot flat dish or individual serving dishes.

Melt 50 g./2 oz. (4 tablespoons) of the butter in a pan, stir in the flour and cook for 2 minutes. Then blend in the milk and the cream and a little of the strained fish liquid. Bring slowly to boiling point and cook until thickened, stirring continually.

Fry the mushrooms in the remaining butter and add to the sauce with the shellfish. Heat gently for 1 to 2 minutes and spoon the sauce over the sole. *Serves 4 to 6*

Sole with savoury butter

Allow one whole sole per person and have them skinned on both sides. Place them in the preheated grill (broiler) pan, heavily brushed with melted butter. Brush the soles with more butter, sprinkle with salt and pepper and grill (broil) for 5 to 6 minutes. Turn the fish over, brush with more butter and grill (broil) for 5 to 6 minutes more. Serve immediately with lemon slices and savoury butter pats. Garnish with parsley.

Crab with black beans

METRIC/IMPERIAL	AMERICAN
2 × 200 g./7 oz. cans crab meat	2 × 7 oz. cans crab meat
25 g./1 oz. black beans	1 oz. black beans
1 garlic clove, crushed	1 garlic clove, crushed
10 ml./2 teaspoons sherry	2 teaspoons sherry
10 ml./2 teaspoons oil	2 teaspoons oil
pinch of ground ginger	pinch of ground ginger

Drain the crab and chop the meat finely; arrange it on the bottom of a greased heatproof dish.

Put the beans in boiling water, bring them back to the boil, then drain them and cool under cold running water. Mash them with a fork. Mix the beans with the garlic, sherry, oil and ginger. Beat the mixture well to make a smooth paste. Spread this mixture over the crab. Cover the dish and steam gently for 45 minutes, then serve in the dish. *Serves 4*

Prawn (shrimp) balls in sweet and sour sauce

Above : Prawn (shrimp) balls in sweet and sour sauce
Below : Grilled (broiled) trout

METRIC/IMPERIAL
100 g./4 oz. self-raising
   flour
salt
1 egg, beaten
150 ml./¼ pint water
½ kg./1 lb. peeled king
   prawns
30 ml./2 tablespoons
   cornflour
2.5 ml./½ teaspoon white
   pepper
pinch of monosodium
   glutamate
peanut oil for deep frying

For the sauce
1 carrot, cut into match-
   stick strips
1 green pepper, cut into
   matchstick strips
2 strips celery stalks, cut
   diagonally
3 tomatoes, skinned and
   chopped
little peanut oil
60 ml./4 tablespoons
   vinegar
60 ml./4 tablespoons sugar
5 ml./1 teaspoon very finely
   chopped fresh ginger
2.5 ml./½ teaspoon salt
7.5 ml./1½ teaspoons
   cornflour

AMERICAN
1 cup self-rising flour
salt
1 egg, beaten
⅝ cup water
1 lb. peeled jumbo prawns
2 tablespoons cornstarch
½ teaspoon white pepper
pinch of monosodium
   glutamate
peanut oil for deep frying

For the sauce
1 carrot, cut into match-
   stick strips
1 green pepper, cut into
   matchstick strips
2 celery stalks, cut
   diagonally
3 tomatoes, skinned and
   chopped
little peanut oil
4 tablespoons vinegar
4 tablespoons sugar
1 teaspoon very finely
   chopped fresh ginger
½ teaspoon salt
1½ teaspoons cornstarch

First cook the fish. Sift the flour and salt into a bowl. Make a well in the centre and add the egg. Using a wooden spoon, mix the flour into the egg, add half the water and continue mixing, drawing in the flour. Beat thoroughly and stir in remaining water. Cut the prawns into chunks about 2.5 cm./ 1 in. across. Mix the cornflour (cornstarch) with salt, pepper and monosodium glutamate. Coat the prawns in this seasoned cornflour (cornstarch), then dip them in the batter and fry in deep, hot oil until crisp and golden. Drain well on absorbent paper and keep hot.

Drop the carrot, green pepper and celery into boiling water and simmer for 5 minutes, then drain. Just cover the base of a pan with peanut oil, heat and put in the vegetables and remaining sauce ingredients. Add 150 ml./¼ pint (⅝ cup) water and bring to the boil, stirring. Add the prawn balls and simmer for 2 minutes. Serve with boiled rice. *Serves 4 to 6*

Grilled (broiled) trout

Allow one trout per person. Have the trout cleaned but see that the heads are left on. Wash the fish and dry on absorbent paper. Place them in a well buttered preheated grill (broiler) pan and brush with melted butter. Grill (broil) for 6 to 8 minutes, depending on thickness. Turn the fish over, brush with more butter and grill (broil) for 6 to 8 minutes more.

Serve immediately, garnished with lemon wedges and parsley. Accompany with extra melted butter.

Mussels marinière

Mussels marinière

METRIC/IMPERIAL
3.5 ml./6 pints fresh
   mussels
25 g./1 oz. butter
4 small onions, chopped
4 parsley sprigs
2 sprigs fresh thyme, or
   1.25 ml./¼ teaspoon
   dried thyme
1 bay leaf
freshly ground black pepper
300 ml./½ pint dry white
   wine
25 g./1 oz. butter
15 ml./1 tablespoon flour
salt
chopped parsley

AMERICAN
4 quarts fresh mussels
2 tablespoons butter
4 small onions, chopped
4 parsley sprigs
2 sprigs fresh thyme, or
   ¼ teaspoon dried thyme
1 bay leaf
freshly ground black pepper
1¼ cups dry white wine
2 tablespoons butter
1 tablespoon flour
salt
chopped parsley

Scrape and clean each mussel with a strong knife, removing every trace of seaweed, mud and beard. Wash very well and discard any mussels which do not close tightly.

Melt the butter in a large pan, add the onions and fry until soft but not coloured. Add the herbs, pepper and wine and then the mussels. Cover with a tightly-fitting lid and cook quickly, shaking the pan constantly, until the mussels open–about 5 to 6 minutes.

Lift the mussels out of the pan, using a slotted spoon, discard the empty half of each shell and keep the mussels hot in a covered serving dish.

Reduce the cooking liquor to about 300 ml./½ pint (1¼ cups). Remove the fresh thyme, parsley sprigs and bay leaf. Blend the butter with the flour and drop it into the simmering stock a teaspoon at a time, whisking until the stock is smooth and thickened. Check the seasoning and add salt if needed. Pour the sauce over the mussels and scatter with plenty of chopped parsley.

Serves 4

*Above : Fish in a jacket ; Above centre : Mixed fried fish ; Above left :
Halibut with egg and lemon sauce*

Fish in a jacket

METRIC/IMPERIAL	AMERICAN
½ kg./1 lb. frozen puff pastry, or pastry made with 225 g./8 oz. flour	1 lb. frozen puff pastry, or pastry made with 2 cups flour
4 large fillets white fish	4 large fillets white fish
salt and pepper	salt and pepper
25 g./1 oz. butter	2 tablespoons butter
25 g./1 oz. flour	¼ cup flour
150 ml./¼ pint milk	⅝ cup milk
100 g./4 oz. mushrooms, chopped	1 cup chopped mushrooms
To glaze	**To glaze**
1 egg, beaten	1 egg, beaten
15 ml./1 tablespoon water	1 tablespoon water
To garnish	**To garnish**
lemon slices	lemon slices
parsley sprigs	parsley sprigs

Roll out the dough thinly and cut into four squares large enough to wrap round the folded fish fillets. Lay the fillets flat on a board and season lightly.

Melt the butter in a pan, add the flour and cook for 2 minutes, stirring. Blend in the milk and slowly bring to the boil; cook until the sauce thickens, stirring continually. Add the mushrooms to the sauce and season well.

Spread the sauce over half of each fillet, then fold the other half over. Lay each fish on a corner of a square of dough. Fold the dough over to form a triangle and seal the edges.

Place the triangles on a baking sheet and brush the tops with the beaten egg mixed with the water. Bake just above the centre of the oven preheated to very hot (240°C/475°F or Gas Mark 9) for 10 minutes, then lower the heat to moderate (180°C/350°F or Gas Mark 4) and cook for 20 to 25 minutes more, or until the pastry is golden brown and well risen. Garnish with lemon slices and parsley sprigs.   *Serves 4*

Mixed fried fish

METRIC/IMPERIAL	AMERICAN
350 g./¾ lb. assorted white fish	¾ lb. assorted white fish
350 g./¾ lb. assorted shellfish	¾ lb. assorted shellfish
flour	flour
hot deep fat or oil	hot deep fat or oil
For the batter	**For the batter**
100 g./4 oz. flour	1 cup flour
good pinch of salt	good pinch of salt
45 ml./3 tablespoons olive oil	3 tablespoons olive oil
225 ml./8 fl. oz. tepid water	1 cup tepid water
1 egg white	1 egg white
To serve	**To serve**
lemon wedges	lemon wedges
tartare sauce	tartare sauce

First prepare the batter. Sift the flour and salt into a bowl. Add the oil and gradually add enough tepid water to make a smooth, creamy batter. Leave to stand in a cool place for 2 hours.

Prepare the fish and cut it into small pieces.

Just before frying, beat the egg white stiffly and fold it into the batter. Dip the pieces of fish in flour, then in the batter. Deep fry in hot fat or oil. Drain well and serve with lemon wedges and tartar sauce. *Serves 4*

Halibut with egg and lemon sauce

METRIC/IMPERIAL	AMERICAN
1 onion, sliced	1 onion, sliced
1 carrot, sliced	1 carrot, sliced
1 slice halibut, about $\frac{1}{2}$ kg./1 lb.	1 slice halibut, about 1 lb.
150 ml./$\frac{1}{4}$ pint water	$\frac{5}{8}$ cup water
salt and pepper	salt and pepper
juice and peeled rind of $\frac{1}{4}$ lemon	juice and peeled rind of $\frac{1}{4}$ lemon
For the sauce	**For the sauce**
10 ml./2 teaspoons cornflour	2 teaspoons cornstarch
1 lemon	1 lemon
1 egg, beaten	1 egg, beaten
To garnish	**To garnish**
$\frac{1}{2}$ cucumber, sliced	$\frac{1}{2}$ cucumber, sliced
1 lemon, sliced	1 lemon, sliced
parsley sprig	parsley sprig

Put the onion and carrot in a shallow pan and place the fish on top. Add the water, seasoning and lemon juice and rind. Cover the pan, bring to the boil, then cook gently for about 15 minutes. When the fish is opaque, it is cooked. Carefully lift out the fish and place it on a heated serving dish. Strain the liquid in the pan for use in the sauce.

To make the sauce, blend the cornflour (cornstarch) with the strained juice of the lemon. Bring the fish liquid to the boil and pour it over the cornflour (cornstarch) mixture. Return the mixture to the pan and cook for 1 minute. Allow the mixture to cool a little, then pour it into a bowl over the beaten egg. Mix and pour the sauce over the fish.

Arrange the cucumber and lemon slices round the fish and garnish with parsley. *Serves 4*

Normandy herrings

METRIC/IMPERIAL	AMERICAN
4 large herrings	4 large herrings
salt and pepper	salt and pepper
25 g./1 oz. flour	¼ cup flour
3 dessert apples	3 dessert apples
75 g./3 oz. butter	⅜ cup butter
1 large onion, chopped	1 large onion, chopped
15 ml./1 tablespoon lemon juice	1 tablespoon lemon juice
parsley sprigs to garnish	parsley sprigs to garnish

Have the fish cleaned and the heads removed. Season the flour and roll the fish in it. Peel, core and chop two of the apples. Heat 50 g./2 oz. (¼ cup) of the butter in a large frying pan. Fry the chopped apples with the onion until the apples are soft and the onion is transparent. Put the mixture in a hot serving dish, sprinkle with the lemon juice and keep warm. Core and slice the remaining apple and fry the slices in the pan.

Heat the remaining butter in the frying pan and fry the fish on each side until tender. Place the fish on top of the apple and onion mixture. Garnish with the apple slices and parsley. *Serves 4*

Left : Normandy herrings
Below left : Tuna fish provençale

Tuna fish provençale

METRIC/IMPERIAL	AMERICAN
2 × 200 g./7 oz. cans tuna fish	2 × 7 oz. cans tuna fish
juice of ½ lemon	juice of ½ lemon
salt and freshly ground black pepper	salt and freshly ground black pepper
4 anchovy fillets	4 anchovy fillets
15 ml./1 tablespoon olive oil	1¼ tablespoons olive oil
1 onion, chopped	1 onion, chopped
4 tomatoes, skinned, seeded and chopped	4 tomatoes, skinned, seeded and chopped
1 garlic clove, crushed	1 garlic clove, crushed
bouquet garni	bouquet garni
150 ml./¼ pint white wine	⅝ cup white wine
chopped parsley for garnish	chopped parsley for garnish

Remove the tuna fish from the cans very carefully so that they stay in shape and place side by side on an ovenproof serving dish. Sprinkle them with lemon juice and season lightly with salt and pepper. Arrange the anchovy fillets on top.

Heat the olive oil in a small pan, add the onion and cook until softened. Add tomatoes, garlic, bouquet garni and wine. Bring to the boil and boil rapidly, uncovered, until reduced and thickened. Pour the sauce over the tuna fish, cover and bake in the oven preheated to moderate (180°C/ 350°F or Gas Mark 4) for 10 to 15 minutes. Remove the bouquet garni and serve sprinkled with chopped parsley. *Serves 4*

Chablis halibut

METRIC/IMPERIAL	AMERICAN
2 wineglasses Chablis or or other dry white wine	2 wineglasses Chablis or other dry white wine
4 halibut steaks	4 halibut cutlets
salt and pepper	salt and pepper
50 g./2 oz. butter	¼ cup butter
To garnish	**To garnish**
hot cooked or canned sweetcorn	hot cooked or canned sweetcorn
red pepper strips	red pepper strips
parsley sprigs	parsley sprigs

Put the wine in a shallow dish and leave the fish soaking in it for 1 hour, turning the fish over after 30 minutes. Lift the fish out of the wine and season lightly. Melt the butter and brush the fish with it. Put the fish in a preheated grill (broiler) pan brushed with melted butter and grill (broil) for about 5 minutes. Turn the fish over, brush with melted butter and grill (broil) for 5 minutes more, or until the fish is cooked through. Serve with the sweetcorn, topped with red pepper, and garnish with parsley. Heat any wine left in the dish and pour it over the fish before serving. *Serves 4*

Above : Chablis halibut
Below : Haddock and mushroom scallops

Haddock and mushroom scallops

METRIC/IMPERIAL	AMERICAN
½ kg./1 lb. potatoes, boiled	1 lb. potatoes, boiled
little butter	little butter
little cream or milk	little cream or milk
225 g./½ lb. fresh haddock	½ lb. fresh haddock
225 g./½ lb. smoked haddock	½ lb. smoked haddock
600 ml./1 pint milk	2½ cups milk
40 g./1½ oz. butter	3 tablespoons butter
25 g./1 oz. flour	¼ cup flour
100 g./4 oz. small button mushrooms	1 cup small button mushrooms
salt and pepper	salt and pepper
1 small can sweetcorn, drained	1 small can sweetcorn, drained
To garnish	**To garnish**
4 tomatoes	4 tomatoes
parsley sprigs	parsley sprigs

Mash the potatoes and mix with a little butter and enough cream or milk to give a soft consistency. Put the potato into a piping bag with a 6 mm./½ in. rose nozzle and pipe a border round six scallop shells or flameproof dishes. Brown gently under a low grill (broiler) while preparing the fish. Put the fish in a pan with the milk and about one-third of the butter. Simmer steadily until tender, about 10 minutes. Lift the fish out of the milk and place it on a flat dish. Allow it to cool slightly, then skin and flake it.

Meanwhile melt the remaining butter in a pan, stir in the flour and cook for 2 minutes. Strain the milk used for the fish into the pan. Bring gradually to the boil and cook until thickened, stirring constantly. Add the mushrooms, seasoning, flaked fish and some of the drained sweetcorn. Put spoonfuls of the fish mixture inside the potato border of each shell or dish. Top with hot sweetcorn. Garnish with wedges of tomato and parsley sprigs. *Serves 6*

Salmon Walewska

Salmon Walewska

METRIC/IMPERIAL
100 g./4 oz. butter
4 salmon cutlets
22.5 ml./1½ tablespoons
  lemon juice
salt and pepper
3 egg yolks
1 small cooked lobster,
  removed from shell and
  diced

To garnish
cucumber slices
lemon wedges
lobster claws

AMERICAN
½ cup butter
4 salmon cutlets
1½ tablespoons lemon juice
salt and pepper
3 egg yolks
1 small cooked lobster,
  removed from shell and
  diced

To garnish
cucumber slices
lemon wedges
lobster claws

Melt 25 g./1 oz. (2 tablespoons) of the butter and brush it over the salmon. Sprinkle with 7.5 ml./½ tablespoon lemon juice and season lightly. Put the salmon in an ovenproof dish, cover with foil, and bake for 20 to 25 minutes in the centre of the oven preheated to moderate (180–190°C/350–375°F or Gas Mark 4–5). The salmon should be just tender; do not overcook.

Put the egg yolks, a little seasoning and the remaining lemon juice in a bowl over a pan of hot water. Whisk until the mixture is thick, then whisk in the remaining butter in small pieces and the diced lobster. Keep warm but do not overheat in case the sauce curdles.

Place the salmon on a hot serving dish, spoon over the sauce and garnish with the cucumber, lemon and lobster claws.   *Serves 4*

Scallops with peppers

METRIC/IMPERIAL
½ kg./1 lb. scallops
15 ml./1 tablespoon oil or
  melted lard
2 spring onions, finely
  chopped
5 ml./1 teaspoon salt
2 green or red peppers,
  seeded and cut into small
  strips
60 ml./4 tablespoons water

AMERICAN
1 lb. scallops
1 tablespoon oil or melted
  lard
2 scallions, finely chopped
1 teaspoon salt
2 green or red peppers,
  seeded and cut into small
  strips
4 tablespoons water

Wash and trim the scallops. Cut each scallop into slices. Heat the oil or lard and fry the scallops and spring onions (scallions) for about 3 minutes, stirring continually. Add the salt and mix well. Add the peppers with the water and bring to the boil, stirring. Then lower the heat and simmer for about 2 minutes. Serve immediately.   *Serves 4*

Scallops Breton-style

METRIC/IMPERIAL	AMERICAN
½ kg./1 lb. scallops	1 lb. scallops
100 g./4 oz. butter, melted	½ cup butter, melted
75 g. 3 oz. fine browned breadcrumbs	¾ cup fine browned breadcrumbs
½ garlic clove, well crushed	½ garlic clove, well crushed
5 ml./1 teaspoon finely chopped parsley	1 teaspoon finely chopped parsley
salt and freshly ground black pepper	salt and freshly ground black pepper
To garnish	**To garnish**
lemon slices	lemon slices
parsley sprigs	parsley sprigs

Trim and wash the scallops. Drain them and cut them into thick pieces. Grease four scallop shells or small ovenproof dishes with a little of the melted butter. Sprinkle with half the breadcrumbs. Divide the sliced scallops equally between the four shells.

Mix the remaining breadcrumbs with the garlic and parsley, and season. Cover the scallops with the breadcrumb mixture and pour over the remaining melted butter. Bake, uncovered, in the oven preheated to warm (170°C/325°F or Gas Mark 3) for 15 to 20 minutes. Serve in the shells or dishes in which they are cooked. Garnish with lemon slices and parsley sprigs. *Serves 4*

Note: If the scallops are large, they may be cooked on skewers as shown in the picture.

Above : Scallops Breton-style
Below : Scallops with peppers

Meat

Swiss veal

Swiss veal

METRIC/IMPERIAL

1½ kg./3 lb. boned leg of
    veal, cut into strips
    5 cm./2 in. long,
    6 mm./¼ in. thick
75 g./3 oz. flour
salt and pepper
175 g./6 oz. butter
2 onions, finely chopped
300 ml./½ pint dry white
225 g./8 oz. mushrooms,
    chopped
300 ml./½ pint dry white
    wine
15 ml./1 tablespoon
    chopped parsley
1.25 ml./¼ teaspoon
    paprika pepper

AMERICAN

3 lb. boned leg of veal, cut
    into strips 2 in. long,
    ¼ in. thick
¾ cup flour
salt and pepper
¾ cup butter
2 onions, finely chopped
1¼ cups dry white wine
8 oz. mushrooms, chopped
1¼ cups cream
1 tablespoon chopped
    parsley
¼ teaspoon paprika pepper

Dip the pieces of veal in seasoned flour. Melt 100 g./4 oz. (½ cup) butter in a frying pan and fry the veal and onions until lightly browned, stirring occasionally. Add the wine and cook over medium heat, stirring to a smooth consistency.

Fry the mushrooms in the remaining butter for 5 minutes.

Then stir in the cream, parsley and paprika. Mix the veal mixture gently with the mushroom mixture and season to taste with salt and pepper. Reheat gently without allowing it to boil. Serve with buttered noodles or sauté potatoes and a mixed or green salad.

Serves 8

Veal mornay

Veal mornay

METRIC/IMPERIAL	AMERICAN
4 small slices ham	4 small slices ham
4 veal escalopes, pounded thin	4 veal cutlets, pounded thin
salt and pepper	salt and pepper
little flour	little flour
1 egg, beaten	1 egg, beaten
100 g./4 oz. dry breadcrumbs	1 cup dry breadcrumbs
50 g./2 oz. butter	$\frac{1}{4}$ cup butter
15 ml./1 tablespoon olive oil	1 tablespoon olive oil
For the sauce	**For the sauce**
25 g./1 oz. butter	2 tablespoons butter
25 g./1 oz. flour	$\frac{1}{4}$ cup flour
150 ml./$\frac{1}{4}$ pint milk	$\frac{5}{8}$ cup milk
150 ml./$\frac{1}{4}$ pint white wine (or use 300 ml./$\frac{1}{2}$ pint milk and omit wine)	$\frac{5}{8}$ cup white wine (or use 1$\frac{1}{4}$ cups milk and omit wine)
5 ml./1 teaspoon French mustard	1 teaspoon French mustard
salt and pepper	salt and pepper
30 ml./2 tablespoons double cream	2 tablespoons heavy cream
100 g./4 oz. Cheddar or Gruyère cheese, grated	1 cup grated Cheddar or Gruyère cheese

For the garnish
boiled new potatoes
chopped parsley
lemon slices
few cooked peas or
    asparagus tips

For the garnish
boiled new potatoes
chopped parsley
lemon slices
few cooked peas or
    asparagus tips

Place the slices of ham so that they cover half of each piece of veal, then fold the veal to cover the ham. Dip the meat in seasoned flour, then in beaten egg and breadcrumbs. Heat the butter and oil together in a large frying pan and fry the veal quickly on each side until crisp and golden brown. Then lower the heat and continue cooking until tender. Lift the meat out of the pan and drain on absorbent paper.

To make the sauce, melt the butter in a pan, then stir in the flour and cook for 2 minutes. Gradually stir in the milk and bring to the boil. Continue cooking, stirring constantly, until the sauce thickens. Then lower the heat and add the wine if used, mustard and salt and pepper. Stir the cream and cheese into the sauce just before serving without allowing the sauce to boil.

Arrange the veal on a dish with a border of new potatoes tossed in parsley. Put a spoonful of sauce in the centre of each piece of meat and top with a twist of lemon and a few peas or asparagus tips. Serve the rest of the sauce separately in a sauce boat.

Serves 4

Veal birds

METRIC/IMPERIAL
2 bacon rashers, chopped
15 ml./1 tablespoon
chopped parsley
1 small garlic clove,
crushed
50 g./2 oz. fresh white
breadcrumbs
1 egg, beaten
½ kg./1 lb. veal escalopes,
pounded thin
25 g./1 oz. butter
15 ml./1 tablespoon flour
150 ml./¼ pint stock or
water
150 ml./¼ pint dry white
wine
salt and pepper
100 g./4 oz. mushrooms,
halved
4 tomatoes, skinned and
quartered
few stuffed green olives

AMERICAN
2 bacon slices, chopped
1 tablespoon chopped
parsley
1 small garlic clove,
crushed
⅔ cup fresh white
breadcrumbs
1 egg, beaten
1 lb. veal cutlets, pounded
thin
2 tablespoons butter
1 tablespoon flour
⅝ cup stock or water
⅝ cup dry white wine
salt and pepper
1 cup halved mushrooms
4 tomatoes, skinned and
quartered
few stuffed green olives

Mix the bacon, parsley, garlic, breadcrumbs and egg. Stuff the slices of veal with this mixture, roll them up tightly and secure with fine string. Melt the butter in a frying pan and fry the veal quickly until browned. Remove the veal from the pan and place in an ovenproof casserole.

Add the flour to the frying pan and cook for 1 minute. Then stir in the water or stock and wine, bring to the boil, add seasoning and pour over the veal. Cover and cook in the oven preheated to warm (170°C/325°F or Gas Mark 3) for 1 hour. Add the remaining ingredients 30 minutes before the end of the cooking time. *Serves 4*

Above left : Veal birds
Above centre : Veal escalope bolognese
Above right : Veal escalopes milanese

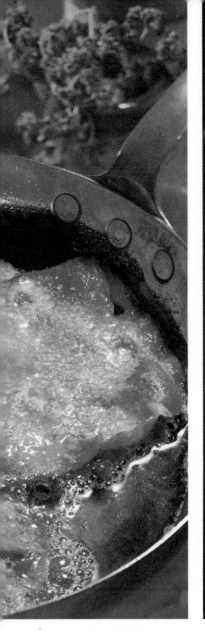

Veal escalopes bolognese

METRIC/IMPERIAL	AMERICAN
4 veal escalopes, pounded thin	4 veal cutlets, pounded thin
flour	flour
salt and pepper	salt and pepper
1 egg, beaten	1 egg, beaten
100 g./4 oz. dry breadcrumbs	1 cup dry breadcrumbs
50 g./2 oz. butter	¼ cup butter
15 ml./1 tablespoon olive oil	1 tablespoon olive oil
4 slices lean ham	4 slices lean ham
grated Parmesan cheese	grated Parmesan cheese
extra butter	extra butter

Coat the veal slices lightly in seasoned flour, then dip them in beaten egg and coat with breadcrumbs. Heat the butter and oil together in a frying pan and fry the veal quickly on each side until golden brown. Return all four escalopes to the pan and cover each with a slice of ham. Then sprinkle with cheese and top with flakes of the extra butter. Cover the pan with a lid and cook for about 3 minutes, or until the cheese melts. Serve immediately. *Serves 4*

Veal escalopes milanese

METRIC/IMPERIAL	AMERICAN
1 egg, beaten	1 egg, beaten
salt and pepper	salt and pepper
4 veal escalopes, pounded thin	4 veal cutlets, pounded thin
100 g./4 oz. dry breadcrumbs	1 cup dry breadcrumbs
50 g./2 oz. butter	¼ cup butter
15 ml./1 tablespoon olive oil	1 tablespoon olive oil
For the garnish	**For the garnish**
1 hardboiled egg, chopped	1 hardcooked egg, chopped
1 lemon, sliced	1 lemon, sliced
parsley sprigs	parsley sprigs

Season the egg with salt and pepper. Dip the escalopes in the egg, then in the breadcrumbs, pressing them on well with a knife.

Melt the butter with the oil in a frying pan. When it is foaming, fry the escalopes for 4 to 5 minutes on each side. Arrange the escalopes on a hot serving dish and garnish with the chopped hardboiled egg, lemon slices and parsley sprigs. *Serves 4*

Veal fricassée

<table>
<tr><td>METRIC/IMPERIAL</td><td>AMERICAN</td></tr>
<tr><td>550 g./1¼ lb. stewing veal, cut into 5 cm./2 in. pieces</td><td>1¼ lb. stewing veal, cut into 2 in. pieces</td></tr>
<tr><td>2 medium onions, finely chopped</td><td>2 medium onions, finely chopped</td></tr>
<tr><td>600 ml./1 pint white stock</td><td>2½ cups white stock</td></tr>
<tr><td>bouquet garni</td><td>bouquet garni</td></tr>
<tr><td>salt and pepper</td><td>salt and pepper</td></tr>
<tr><td>50 g./2 oz. butter</td><td>¼ cup butter</td></tr>
<tr><td>50 g./2 oz. flour</td><td>½ cup flour</td></tr>
<tr><td>2 egg yolks</td><td>2 egg yolks</td></tr>
<tr><td>30 ml./2 tablespoons lemon juice</td><td>2 tablespoons lemon juice</td></tr>
<tr><td>150 ml./¼ pint double cream</td><td>⅝ cup heavy cream</td></tr>
<tr><td>**For the garnish**</td><td>**For the garnish**</td></tr>
<tr><td>4 bacon rashers</td><td>4 bacon slices</td></tr>
<tr><td>6–8 slices of bread</td><td>6–8 slices of bread</td></tr>
<tr><td>1–2 lemons</td><td>1–2 lemons</td></tr>
<tr><td>parsley sprigs</td><td>parsley sprigs</td></tr>
</table>

Put the veal and the onions in a pan and add nearly all the stock. Bring the stock to the boil, remove any scum that comes to the surface and add the bouquet garni and seasoning. Cover the pan and simmer very slowly for 1½ hours. When the veal is tender, add the butter. Mix the flour with the remaining stock and add it to the veal liquid, stirring. Bring to the boil and cook steadily, stirring constantly, until the sauce thickens. Remove the bouquet garni.

Mix the egg yolks with the lemon juice and cream. Take the pan of veal off the heat and stir in the egg and cream mixture. Return the pan to the heat and simmer for 5 minutes, stirring constantly. Take care not to let the sauce boil.

Remove the bacon rinds and cut the rashers (slices) in half. Stretch them with the back of a knife and roll them. Put the bacon rolls on a skewer and grill (broil). Toast the bread, remove the crusts and cut the toast into triangles.

Spoon the veal and sauce on to a hot serving dish and top with bacon rolls, triangles of lemon and parsley sprigs. Arrange the toast round the edge of the dish. Serve extra toast and lemon with the veal. *Serves 4*

Veal escalopes, Turin-style

<table>
<tr><td>METRIC/IMPERIAL</td><td>AMERICAN</td></tr>
<tr><td>4 veal escalopes, pounded thin</td><td>4 veal cutlets, pounded thin</td></tr>
<tr><td>flour</td><td>flour</td></tr>
<tr><td>salt and pepper</td><td>salt and pepper</td></tr>
<tr><td>1 egg, beaten</td><td>1 egg, beaten</td></tr>
<tr><td>50 g./2 oz. dry breadcrumbs</td><td>½ cup dry breadcrumbs</td></tr>
<tr><td>50 g./2 oz. grated Parmesan cheese</td><td>½ cup grated Parmesan cheese</td></tr>
<tr><td>50 g./2 oz. butter</td><td>50 g./2 oz. butter</td></tr>
<tr><td>15 ml./1 tablespoon olive oil</td><td>1 tablespoon olive oil</td></tr>
<tr><td>**For the garnish**</td><td>**For the garnish**</td></tr>
<tr><td>4 tomato slices</td><td>4 tomato slices</td></tr>
<tr><td>4 anchovy fillets</td><td>4 anchovy fillets</td></tr>
<tr><td>lemon wedges</td><td>lemon wedges</td></tr>
</table>

Coat the veal lightly in seasoned flour, then dip the pieces of meat in beaten egg. Mix the breadcrumbs and grated cheese and coat the meat in this mixture. Heat the butter and oil together and fry the veal on both sides until golden brown and tender. Top each escalope (scallop) with a tomato slice and an anchovy fillet. Garnish with lemon wedges. *Serves 4*

Opposite left : Veal fricassée
Centre : Veal escalopes Turin-style
Above : Beef bourguignonne

Beef bourguignonne

METRIC/IMPERIAL	AMERICAN
2 kg./4 lb. topside or rump steak, cubed	4 lb. round or sirloin steak, cubed
50 g./2 oz. flour	½ cup flour
60 ml./4 tablespoons olive oil	4 tablespoons olive oil
100 g./4 oz. butter	½ cup butter
225 g./8 oz. bacon or pork, diced	8 oz. bacon or pork, diced
90 ml./6 tablespoons brandy (optional)	6 tablespoons brandy (optional)
4 carrots, chopped	4 carrots, chopped
2 leeks, sliced	2 leeks, sliced
2 onions, chopped	2 onions, chopped
2 garlic cloves, crushed	2 garlic cloves, crushed
1 bouquet garni	1 bouquet garni
20 ml./4 teaspoons salt	4 teaspoons salt
freshly ground black pepper	freshly ground black pepper
600 ml./1 pint red Burgundy wine	2½ cups red Burgundy wine
600 ml./1 pint beef stock	2½ cups beef stock
30 ml./2 tablespoons cornflour	2 tablespoons cornstarch
24 small pickling onions	24 small pickling onions
24 button mushrooms	24 button mushrooms
extra oil and butter for frying	extra oil and butter for frying
juice of 1 large lemon	juice of 1 large lemon
chopped parsley to garnish	chopped parsley to garnish

Roll the cubes of beef in the flour. Heat the oil and butter together in a large heavy frying pan. Fry the bacon or pork until crisp, then transfer it to a large flameproof casserole. Fry the meat in several batches until it is browned all over. If using brandy, heat it, set light to it and add it flaming to the meat. Then transfer the meat and juices to the casserole.

Fry the carrots, leeks, onions and garlic until golden, then transfer them to the casserole. Add the bouquet garni, salt, pepper and wine to the casserole. Add the stock to the frying pan and heat, stirring to loosen the sediment, then transfer to the casserole. Cover the casserole and cook in the oven preheated to warm (170°C/325°F or Gas Mark 3) for 1½ to 2 hours. Remove the bouquet garni.

Mix the cornflour (cornstarch) with 30 ml./2 tablespoons cold water to a smooth paste. Stir it into the casserole and bring back to boiling point on top of the stove to thicken the sauce.

Fry the onions and mushrooms in extra oil and butter, add lemon juice and simmer until tender. Add to the casserole and serve sprinkled with parsley.

Note: Beef bourguignonne is usually thickened with a flour and butter paste but blended cornflour (cornstarch) is more suitable for a large quantity. The dish may be cooked completely the night before it is needed. It should be cooled, covered and stored in the refrigerator, then reheated the next day for serving.

Serves 10 to 12

Carpetbag steaks

Carpetbag steaks

METRIC/IMPERIAL
6 thick pieces of fillet or
   rump steak
about 24 washed and
   cooked mussels, or
   shelled and sliced
   oysters
100 g./4 oz. butter, melted
15 ml./1 tablespoon
   chopped parsley
lemon juice
salt and pepper
For the garnish
tomatoes
mushrooms
parsley sprigs

AMERICAN
6 thick pieces of tenderloin
   or round steak
about 24 washed and
   cooked mussels, or
   shelled and sliced
   oysters
½ cup butter
1 tablespoon chopped
   parsley
lemon juice
salt and pepper
For the garnish
tomatoes
mushrooms
parsley sprigs

Split the steaks to make 'pockets'. Mix the mussels or oysters with half the butter, the chopped parsley, a squeeze of lemon juice and seasoning. Put the mixture in the 'pockets' of the steak and skewer firmly or sew with fine string or cotton. Brush the steaks with the remaining butter and grill (broil) to taste until tender. Remove the skewers or string or cotton and serve garnished with grilled (broiled) tomatoes, fried mushrooms and parsley sprigs. *Serves 6*

Steak and kidney pie

Steak and kidney pie

METRIC/IMPERIAL
225 g./8 oz. quantity flaky
   pastry dough
1 egg to glaze
For the filling
700 g./1½ lb. braising steak,
   cubed
225 g./8 oz. ox kidneys,
   skinned, cored and sliced
25 g./1 oz. flour
salt and pepper
50 g./2 oz. dripping or fat
400 ml./¾ pint beef stock

AMERICAN
2 cup quantity flaky
   pastry dough
1 egg to glaze
For the filling
1½ lb. round steak, cubed
8 oz. ox kidneys, skinned,
   cored and sliced
¼ cup flour
salt and pepper
¼ cup dripping or fat
2 cups beef stock

Roll the meat and kidneys in seasoned flour and fry gently in hot dripping or fat. Gradually stir in the stock. Bring to the boil and cook until the stock has thickened, stirring constantly. Lower the heat, cover the pan tightly and cook gently until almost tender, about 2 to 2½ hours. Make sure the liquid does not evaporate too much and add more if necessary.

Spoon the meat and a little gravy into a pie dish of 2.4 to 2.8 l./2½ to 3 pints (6¼ to 7½ cups) capacity and allow to cool.

Roll out the dough and trim off a strip to go round the edge of the pie dish. Dampen the strip and cover the dish with dough. Trim off excess dough with a knife and make indentations at regular intervals round the edge. Make a slit in the centre of the pie and decorate with leaves made from the trimmings. Brush with beaten egg mixed with a little water. Bake in the centre of the oven preheated to very hot (230°C/450°F or Gas Mark 8) for 15 minutes, then lower the heat to moderate (180°C/350°F or Gas Mark 4) and cook for 30 to 35 minutes, or until the pastry is brown and firm.

Serves 6

Beef and prune stew

METRIC/IMPERIAL	AMERICAN
550 g./1¼ lb. chuck steak, cubed	1¼ lb. chuck steak, cubed
salt and pepper	salt and pepper
25 g./1 oz. flour	¼ cup flour
50 g./2 oz. fat or dripping	¼ cup fat or dripping
15 ml./1 tablespoon tomato puree	1 tablespoon tomato purée
about 18 prunes, soaked overnight in 600 ml./ 1 pint brown stock	about 18 prunes, soaked overnight in 2½ cups brown stock
2 bay leaves	2 bay leaves
4 tomatoes, skinned	4 tomatoes, skinned

Roll the meat in seasoned flour and cook in the hot fat or dripping until it is browned all over. Strain the stock from the prunes and add it to the meat. Bring to the boil and cook until the stock has thickened. Add the tomato purée, about six finely-chopped stoned prunes and the bay leaves. Cover the pan and simmer for 1¾ hours. Add the rest of the prunes, whole, and cook for 15 minutes more. Then add the tomatoes and cook for another 15 minutes. Remove the bay leaves.

Serves 4

Steak upside-down pie

METRIC/IMPERIAL	AMERICAN
2 onions, chopped	2 onions, chopped
2–3 tomatoes, skinned and chopped	2–3 tomatoes, skinned and chopped
few mushrooms or mushroom stalks, chopped	few mushrooms or mushroom stalks, chopped
50 g./2 oz. dripping	¼ cup dripping
300 ml./½ pint beef stock	1¼ cups beef stock
350 g./12 oz. minced beef	12 oz. ground beef
parsley sprigs to garnish	parsley sprigs to garnish
For the topping	**For the topping**
175 g./6 oz. self-raising flour	1½ cups self-rising flour
salt and pepper	salt and pepper
50 g./2 oz. butter or fat	¼ cup butter or fat
50 g./2 oz. Cheddar cheese, grated	½ cup grated Cheddar cheese
1 egg yolk	1 egg yolk
milk to mix	milk to mix

Fry the vegetables in hot dripping until soft. Add the stock and the minced (ground) beef. Stir until smooth and thick and season well. Cook for 15 minutes, uncovered, stirring occasionally.

Meanwhile prepare the topping. Sift the flour with seasoning. Rub in the butter or fat and stir in the grated cheese. Bind with the egg yolk and add enough milk to give a soft rolling consistency. Form the dough into a round about

17.5 cm./7 in. in diameter. Put the meat mixture in a cake tin or ovenproof dish and top with the dough. Bake in the centre of the oven preheated to moderate (180°C/350°F or Gas Mark 4) for about 50 minutes. Invert on to a hot dish and garnish with parsley. Serve with creamed carrots and potatoes.   *Serves 4*

Opposite left : Beef and prune stew
Centre : Steak upside-down pie
Above : Stuffed fillet of beef

Stuffed fillet of beef

METRIC/IMPERIAL	AMERICAN
3 onions, sliced	3 onions, sliced
beef dripping	beef dripping
4 anchovy fillets, chopped	4 anchovy fillets, chopped
30 ml./2 tablespoons finely chopped bacon	2 tablespoons finely chopped bacon
pinch of pepper	pinch of pepper
pinch of dried thyme	pinch of dried thyme
pinch of finely chopped parsley	pinch of finely chopped parsley
1 egg yolk	1 egg yolk
1 kg./2 lb. beef fillet	2 lb. beef fillet
watercress sprigs to garnish	watercress sprigs to garnish

Fry the onions in about 15 ml./1 tablespoon dripping until golden brown. Remove them from the pan and place them in a mixing bowl. Add the anchovy fillets, bacon, pepper, herbs and egg yolk to the onion and mix well. Cut the fillet in about six places, but not right through. Put some of the stuffing in each cavity and tie the fillet with clean string or secure with wooden toothpicks. Wrap in greased foil or place in a covered roasting pan with a little dripping and cook in the oven preheated to warm (170°C/325°F or Gas Mark 3) for 1½ hours or until tender. Cut into thick slices to serve and garnish with watercress sprigs.   *Serves 4*

Braised beef whirls

METRIC/IMPERIAL
1 onion, finely chopped
175 g./6 oz. ox kidney,
   skinned, cored and finely
   chopped
15 ml./1 tablespoon
   chopped parsley
25 g./1 oz. margarine or
   shredded suet
salt and pepper
4 slices beef topside,
   halved
2 onions, sliced
6 carrots, sliced
50 g./2 oz. dripping
25 g./1 oz. flour
300 ml./½ pint beef stock
chopped parsley to garnish

AMERICAN
1 onion, finely chopped
6 oz. ox kidney, skinned,
   cored and finely
   chopped
1 tablespoon chopped
   parsley
2 tablespoons margarine or
   shredded suet
salt and pepper
4 slices top round
   of beef, halved
2 onions, sliced
6 carrots, sliced
¼ cup dripping
¼ cup flour
1¼ cups beef stock
chopped parsley to garnish

Mix the chopped onion, kidney, chopped parsley, margarine or suet and seasoning. Divide the mixture between the pieces of meat and roll up firmly. Secure with wooden toothpicks or string. Put the sliced onions and carrots in an ovenproof casserole.

Heat the dripping in a frying pan. Coat the beef rolls in seasoned flour and fry them quickly in the dripping until browned all over. Place the beef rolls on top of the vegetables in the casserole. Blend the stock with the juices in the frying pan and pour it round the meat. Cover the casserole and cook in the coolest part of the oven preheated to warm (170°C/325°F or Gas Mark 3) for about 1½ hours, or until the meat is tender. Sprinkle with chopped parsley before serving.

Serves 4

Beef and vegetable stew

METRIC/IMPERIAL	AMERICAN
550 g./1¾ lb. chuck steak, cubed	1¾ lb. chuck steak, cubed
25 g./1 oz. flour	¼ cup flour
salt and pepper	salt and pepper
50 g./2 oz. dripping or fat	¼ cup dripping or fat
8 small onions	8 small onions
600 ml./1 pint brown stock	2½ cups brown stock
8 small carrots	8 small carrots
2–3 celery stalks	2–3 celery stalks
100 g./4 oz. button mushrooms	1 cup button mushrooms
bouquet garni	bouquet garni
chopped parsley to garnish	chopped parsley to garnish

Roll the meat in seasoned flour. Melt the fat in a large pan and quickly cook the meat and onions for a few minutes, turning the meat until it is browned all over. Stir in the stock gradually. Bring the liquid to the boil and stir well until it has thickened slightly. Add the remaining vegetables, leaving the carrots and mushrooms whole, and the bouquet garni. Season to taste and cover with a well-fitting lid. Simmer for 2¼ to 2½ hours, or until the meat is tender.

Remove the bouquet garni and serve in a hot dish. Garnish with chopped parsley.   *Serves 4*

Beef curry

METRIC/IMPERIAL	AMERICAN
15 ml./1 tablespoon ground coriander	1 tablespoon ground coriander
5 ml./1 teaspoon ground turmeric	1 teaspoon ground turmeric
2.5 ml./½ teaspoon cumin	½ teaspoon cumin
1.25 ml./¼ teaspoon chilli powder	¼ teaspoon chili powder
pinch of ground cinnamon	pinch of ground cinnamon
2 cloves	2 cloves
45 ml./3 tablespoons vinegar	3 tablespoons vinegar
30 ml./2 tablespoons vegetable oil	2 tablespoons vegetable oil
1 onion, chopped	1 onion, chopped
1 garlic clove, crushed	1 garlic clove, crushed
½ kg./1 lb. beef topside	1 lb. top round of beef
5 ml./1 teaspoon salt	1 teaspoon salt
150 ml./¼ pint beef stock	⅝ cup beef stock
1 bay leaf	1 bay leaf
orange wedges to garnish	orange wedges to garnish
boiled rice to serve	boiled rice to serve

Mix and pound the spices with the vinegar to form a paste. Heat the oil in a heavy pan and fry the onion and garlic gently for 5 minutes. Add the curry paste and fry for 2 to 3 minutes, stirring constantly. Add the beef and cook gently, stirring occasionally, until it browns. Add salt, stock and bay leaf, cover and simmer for 1 hour. Remove the bay leaf, taste the curry and adjust the seasoning if necessary. Garnish with orange wedges.

Serve with boiled rice and chutney.   *Serves 4*

Opposite : Braised beef whirls
Below : Beef and vegetable stew
Below right : Beef curry

Pepperpot beef

METRIC/IMPERIAL	AMERICAN
25 g./1 oz. flour	¼ cup flour
5 ml./1 teaspoon salt	1 teaspoon salt
pinch of pepper	pinch of pepper
2.5 ml./½ teaspoon ground ginger	½ teaspoon ground ginger
1 kg./2 lb. braising beef, cubed	2 lb. round steak, cubed
50 g./2 oz. lard or dripping	¼ cup lard or dripping
1 small red pepper, diced	1 small red pepper, diced
1 × 425 g./15 oz. can red kidney beans, drained	1 × 15 oz. can red kidney beans, drained

For the sauce

5 ml./1 teaspoon chilli sauce	1 teaspoon chili sauce
1 × 225 g./8 oz. can tomatoes	1 × 8 oz. can tomatoes
100 g./4 oz. mushrooms, sliced	1 cup sliced mushrooms
15 ml./1 tablespoon Worcestershire sauce	1 tablespoon Worcestershire sauce
30 ml./2 tablespoons wine vinegar	2 tablespoons wine vinegar
2 garlic cloves, crushed	2 garlic cloves, crushed
1 bay leaf	1 bay leaf

Mix the flour, seasoning and ginger and coat the beef cubes with it. Melt the lard or dripping in a large frying pan and quickly fry the beef until it is browned, turning once. Drain on absorbent paper, then transfer it to an ovenproof casserole.

Combine all the ingredients for the sauce and pour it over the meat. Cover and cook in the oven preheated to warm (170°C/325°F or Gas Mark 3) for about 2 hours or until the meat is tender. Add the red pepper and kidney beans 30 minutes before the end of the cooking time. *Serves 6*

Hamburgers

METRIC/IMPERIAL	AMERICAN
½ kg./1 lb. minced lean beef	1 lb. ground lean beef
1 egg or egg yolk	1 egg or egg yolk
salt and pepper	salt and pepper
pinch of dried mixed herbs	pinch of dried mixed herbs
flour	flour
fat for frying	fat for frying
4 soft rolls or baps	4 hamburger buns

Mix the meat, egg or egg yolk, seasoning and herbs. Form the mixture into four flat cakes (patties) with floured hands. Fry in a little hot fat for 3 to 4 minutes on each side. Serve in the rolls.

Hamburgers may be served with tomato ketchup, onion rings, horseradish, chutney and any other relishes of your choice. *Serves 4*

Below left : Pepperpot beef
Below : Hamburgers
Above : Killarney hot-pot

Killarney hot-pot

METRIC/IMPERIAL	AMERICAN
700 g./1½ lb. potatoes, sliced	1½ lb. potatoes, sliced
salt and pepper	salt and pepper
½ kg./1 lb. onions, sliced	1 lb. onions, sliced
2–3 large carrots, sliced	2–3 large carrots, sliced
225 g./8 oz. belly of pork or fat ham, diced	8 oz. belly of pork or fat ham, diced
½ kg./1 lb. lean brisket or chuck steak, cubed	1 lb. lean brisket or chuck steak, cubed
1.25 ml./¼ teaspoon dried sage	¼ teaspoon dried sage
150 ml./¼ pint brown ale	⅝ cup dark beer
25 g./1 oz. butter	2 tablespoons butter

Put one-third of the potatoes in an ovenproof casserole and season well. Then put in half the onions, carrots and meat, seasoning each layer, and sprinkle a little sage over the meat. Put in another layer of potatoes, keeping some for the top, and the remaining onions, carrots and meat. Season each layer and sprinkle the meat with sage. Pour over the beer, then arrange the remaining potatoes on top and dot with butter.

Cook for 2 hours in the centre of the oven preheated to warm (170°C/325°F or Gas Mark 3). Leave the casserole uncovered for the first 15 minutes of cooking so that the butter melts and coats the potatoes. Then remove the lid 20 minutes before the end of cooking to brown the potatoes.

Serves 4 to 5

Pork and bamboo shoots

Pork and bamboo shoots

METRIC/IMPERIAL
45 ml./3 tablespoons soy
  sauce
15 ml./1 tablespoon sherry
5 ml./1 teaspoon brown
  sugar
5 ml./1 teaspoon ground
  ginger
1 kg./2 lb. lean pork,
  cubed
1.1 l./2 pints water
100 g./4 oz. bamboo shoots,
  drained and shredded

AMERICAN
3 tablespoons soy sauce
1 tablespoon sherry
1 teaspoon brown sugar
1 teaspoon ground ginger
2 lb. lean pork, cubed
5 cups water
4 oz. bamboo shoots,
  drained and shredded

Mix the soy sauce, sherry, sugar and ginger in a bowl. Add
the pork cubes, toss them well and leave to marinate for 10
minutes.

Put the pork and marinade into a large pan, add the water
and bring gently to the boil, then cover and simmer for
1 hour. Add the bamboo shoots and simmer for 10 minutes.
Serve immediately. *Serves 6 to 8*
Note: The liquid may be thickened slightly with 15 ml./
1 tablespoon cornflour (cornstarch) mixed to a smooth paste
with a little cold water.

Ham and sweet peppers

METRIC/IMPERIAL
3 red peppers, shredded
15 ml./1 tablespoon
  cornflour
30 ml./2 tablespoons soy
  sauce
15 ml./1 tablespoon sherry
5 ml./1 teaspoon sugar
30 ml./2 tablespoons stock
  or water
350 g./12 oz. ham, cubed
30 ml./2 tablespoons oil

AMERICAN
3 red peppers, shredded
1 tablespoon cornstarch
2 tablespoons soy sauce
1 tablespoon sherry
1 teaspoon sugar
2 tablespoons stock or water
12 oz. ham, cubed
2 tablespoons oil

Cover the shredded peppers with boiling water and leave for
1 minute to blanch, then drain. Mix the cornflour (cornstarch), soy sauce, sherry, sugar and stock or water. Pour the
mixture over the ham and mix well so that the meat is completely coated. Heat the oil in a frying pan and fry the
peppers for 2 minutes over fierce heat, stirring constantly.
Remove the peppers from the pan. Put the ham into the pan,
with the liquid, and cook for 1 minute, stirring constantly,
over medium heat. Add the peppers, cook for another
minute, then serve. *Serves 4*

Above : Ham and sweet peppers; Below : Normandy pork

Normandy pork

METRIC/IMPERIAL	AMERICAN
5–6 thick pork chops	5–6 thick pork chops
fat for frying	fat for frying
2 onions, chopped	2 onions, chopped
300 ml./½ pint white wine	1¼ cups white wine
15 ml./1 tablespoon	1 tablespoon Calvados
Calvados (optional)	(optional)
pinch of sage	pinch of sage
2–3 dessert apples, peeled,	2–3 dessert apples, peeled,
cored and chopped	cored and chopped
salt and pepper	salt and pepper
little olive oil	little olive oil

Fry the chops in hot fat in a large frying pan for 5 to 8 minutes, or until lightly browned. Lift them out of the pan. Fry the onions in the pan until tender but not brown. Add the wine, Calvados, if used, sage, apples and seasoning. Put the mixture in a large ovenproof casserole and put the chops on top. Keep the skin uppermost so that it crisps and brush with oil. Do not cover the dish. Cook for 40 to 45 minutes in the centre of the oven preheated to moderate (180°C/350°F or Gas Mark 4). *Serves 5 to 6*

Gammon (ham) with pineapple and corn sauce

METRIC/IMPERIAL	AMERICAN
4 gammon slices	4 ham slices
50 g./2 oz. butter, melted	¼ cup butter, melted
4 rings of canned pineapple	4 rings of canned pineapple
watercress to garnish	watercress to garnish
For the sauce	**For the sauce**
25 g./1 oz. butter	2 tablespoons butter
25 g./1 oz. flour	¼ cup flour
300 ml./½ pint milk	1¼ cups milk
1 onion, finely chopped	1 onion, finely chopped
salt and pepper	salt and pepper
60 ml./4 tablespoons cooked or canned sweetcorn	4 tablespoons cooked or canned sweetcorn
10 ml./2 teaspoons chopped parsley	2 teaspoons chopped parsley
30 ml./2 tablespoons syrup from pineapple	2 tablespoons syrup from pineapple

Snip the edges of the gammon (ham) to prevent it curling. Brush the gammon (ham) with melted butter and grill (broil) for several minutes, then turn it, brush with more butter and grill (broil) for several minutes on the other side. When the gammon (ham) is almost cooked, brush the pineapple rings with melted butter and put them on the grill (broiler) pan to heat.

While the gammon (ham) is cooking, make the sauce. Melt the butter in a pan, add the flour and cook for 2 minutes, stirring constantly. Gradually blend in the milk, still stirring, and add the onion. Bring the sauce to the boil and cook until it has thickened, stirring constantly. Season the sauce and add the sweetcorn and parsley. When ready to serve, whisk in the pineapple syrup.

Arrange the gammon (ham) on a hot serving dish and put the pineapple slices on top. Garnish with watercress and serve the sauce separately. *Serves 4*

Sweet and sour pork with lychees

METRIC/IMPERIAL	AMERICAN
45 ml./3 tablespoons soy sauce	3 tablespoons soy sauce
15 ml./1 tablespoon dry sherry	1 tablespoon dry sherry
5 ml./1 teaspoon very finely chopped fresh ginger	1 teaspoon very finely chopped fresh ginger
pinch of monosodium glutamate	pinch of monosodium glutamate
½ kg./1 lb. spring or shoulder pork, cubed	1 lb. picnic shoulder pork, cubed
25 g./1 oz. flour	¼ cup flour
25 g./1 oz. cornflour	¼ cup cornstarch
pinch of salt	pinch of salt
2 eggs, beaten	2 eggs, beaten
oil for deep frying	oil for deep frying
½ red pepper, cut into wedges	½ red pepper, cut into wedges
½ green pepper, cut into wedges	½ green pepper, cut into wedges
2 apples, peeled, cored and quartered	2 apples, peeled, cored and quartered
15 ml./1 tablespoon brown sugar	1 tablespoon brown sugar
150 ml./¼ pint syrup from canned lychees	⅝ cup syrup from canned lychees
30 ml./2 tablespoons vinegar	2 tablespoons vinegar
4 spring onions, finely chopped	4 scallions, finely chopped
1 × 300 g./11 oz. can lychees, drained	1 × 11 oz. can lychees, drained
extra 15 ml./1 tablespoon cornflour	extra 1 tablespoon cornstarch
extra 15 ml./1 tablespoon soy sauce	extra 1 tablespoon soy sauce
salt to taste	salt to taste

Mix in a bowl the soy sauce, sherry, ginger and monosodium glutamate. Add the pork cubes, stir to coat them and marinate for 1 to 2 hours.

Sift the flour, cornflour (cornstarch) and salt into a bowl. Add the eggs gradually, beating well to make a smooth batter. Coat the pork cubes in the batter and deep fry them in hot oil until golden. Drain them on absorbent paper and keep hot.

Mix all the remaining ingredients in a small pan. Bring to the boil, stirring constantly, and simmer for 2 to 3 minutes. Put the pork on a heated serving dish and pour over the sauce. Serve immediately. *Serves 4 to 6*

Gammon (ham) with pineapple and corn sauce

Stuffed ham rolls

METRIC/IMPERIAL	AMERICAN
2 celery stalks, chopped	2 celery stalks, chopped
2 apples, peeled, cored and chopped	2 apples, peeled, cored and chopped
50 g./2 oz. chopped walnuts	$\frac{1}{2}$ cup chopped walnuts
15 ml./1 tablespoon chopped chives	1 tablespoon chopped chives
15 ml./1 tablespoon lemon juice	1 tablespoon lemon juice
150 ml./$\frac{1}{4}$ pint mayonnaise	$\frac{5}{8}$ cup mayonnaise
salt and pepper	salt and pepper
8 ham slices	8 ham slices
100 g./4 oz. pâté	4 oz. pâté
For the garnish	**For the garnish**
parsley sprigs	parsley sprigs
lemon slices	lemon slices

Above : Sweet and sour pork with lychees
Below : Stuffed ham rolls

Mix the celery, apples, walnuts, chives and lemon juice. Add the mayonnaise, then taste and adjust seasoning. Spread each slice of ham with pâté. Divide the mayonnaise mixture between the slices and roll them up. Garnish with parsley and lemon.

Serves 4

Above : Loin of lamb with haricot beans ; Above right : Roast lamb with apricot nut stuffing

Loin of lamb with haricot beans

METRIC/IMPERIAL
225 g./8 oz. haricot beans,
 soaked overnight
 and drained
salt
1 carrot
1 onion
bouquet garni
1 kg./2 lb. loin of lamb,
 boned
1 garlic clove
300 ml./½ pint brown stock
2 large tomatoes, skinned,
 seeded and chopped
parsley to garnish

AMERICAN
1⅓ cups lima or navy beans,
 soaked overnight and
 drained
salt
1 carrot
1 onion
bouquet garni
2 lb. loin of lamb, boned
1 garlic clove
1¼ cups brown stock
2 large tomatoes, skinned,
 seeded and chopped
parsley to garnish

Place the beans in a large saucepan with salted cold water to cover. Add the carrot, onion and bouquet garni. Bring to the boil and simmer for 2 hours, or until tender.

Meanwhile, wipe the lamb and rub it all over with salt. Place slivers of garlic in various places under the skin of the lamb. Roll the meat and tie with fine string. Place the lamb in a greased roasting pan with the stock, cover with greased greaseproof (waxed) paper and roast in the oven preheated to fairly hot (190°C/375°F or Gas Mark 5) for 50 minutes. After 20 minutes remove the paper and baste with the stock in the pan, then replace the paper. Baste two or three more times during cooking and remove the paper for the last 10 minutes to brown.

Place the meat on a heated serving dish and keep it hot. Drain the cooked beans. Remove the onion and carrot and chop. Mix the beans with the tomatoes, carrot and onion and a little of the meat stock to moisten. Spoon the beans around the meat and garnish with parsley. *Serves 4*

Roast lamb with apricot nut stuffing

METRIC/IMPERIAL
boned shoulder or loin of
 lamb
25–50 g./1–2 oz. fat
For the stuffing
1 medium can apricots,
 drained and chopped
75 g./3 oz. fresh
 breadcrumbs
50 g./2 oz. chopped walnuts
50 g./2 oz. softened butter
juice of 1 orange and
 1 lemon
salt and pepper
1 egg, beaten

AMERICAN
boned shoulder or loin
 of lamb
2–4 tablespoons fat
For the stuffing
1 medium can apricots,
 drained and chopped
1 cup fresh breadcrumbs
½ cup chopped walnuts
¼ cup softened butter
juice of 1 orange and
 1 lemon
salt and pepper
1 egg, beaten

Combine all the ingredients for the stuffing and moisten with a little juice from the apricots if necessary. Spread the stuffing over the meat, roll up and tie with fine string. Weigh the meat to calculate cooking time.

Put the meat in a roasting pan and spread fat over it. Cook in the oven preheated to hot (220°C/425°F or Gas Mark 7) for 15 minutes, then lower the heat to 190°C/375°F or Gas Mark 5. Allow 20 minutes per 450 g./1 lb. and 20 minutes over (slightly less if you like the meat pink). For slow roasting, set the oven at moderate (180°C/350°F or Gas Mark 4) and cook for 35 minutes per 450 g./1 lb. and 35 minutes over. Serve with thin gravy and mint sauce. *Serves 6*

Simple cassoulet

METRIC/IMPERIAL
30 ml./2 tablespoons bacon
   fat
700 g./1½ lb. stewing lamb,
   cubed
2 onions, sliced
400 ml./¾ pint water or
   stock
1 × 150 g./5 oz. can
   tomato purée
175 g./6 oz. haricot beans,
   soaked overnight and
   drained
2 carrots, sliced
1 parsnip, sliced
1 celery stalk, sliced
parsley sprig
pinch of dried thyme
1 bay leaf
freshly ground black pepper
salt

AMERICAN
2 tablespoons bacon fat
1½ lb. stewing lamb, cubed
2 onions, sliced
2 cups water or stock
1 × 5 oz. can tomato purée
1 cup lima or navy beans,
   soaked overnight and
   drained
2 carrots, sliced
1 parsnip, sliced
1 celery stalk, sliced
parsley sprig
pinch of dried thyme
1 bay leaf
freshly ground black pepper
salt

Melt the fat in a large, heavy pan and cook the lamb and onions until the lamb is lightly browned and the onions transparent. Pour in a little water or stock and stir in the tomato purée. Add the rest of the water or stock, the beans, carrots, parsnip, celery, herbs and pepper to taste and stir well.

Bring gently to the boil, then cover and simmer until the meat is very tender, about 2 hours. Add salt to taste and simmer gently for 30 minutes more, uncovered.   *Serves 4*

Kebabs

METRIC/IMPERIAL
½ kg./1 lb. lean lamb or
    pork, cubed
good pinch of ground
    allspice
salt and pepper
4 onions, quartered
8 tomatoes, halved or
    quartered
2 green peppers, cut in
    large pieces
oil
For serving
225 g./8 oz. long grain rice
30 ml./2 tablespoons oil
600 ml./1 pint stock

AMERICAN
1 lb. lean lamb or pork,
    cubed
good pinch of ground
    allspice
salt and pepper
4 onions, quartered
8 tomatoes, halved or
    quartered
2 green peppers, cut in
    large pieces
oil
For serving
1¼ cups long grain rice
2 tablespoons oil
2½ cups stock

Toss the rice in hot oil, then add the stock and cook until the
stock is absorbed and the rice is tender.

While the rice is cooking, prepare the kebabs. Roll the
meat in the allspice and seasoning. Arrange the meat, onions,
tomatoes and peppers alternately on the skewers. Brush
them with oil and grill (broil), turning them while they cook
so that the meat browns evenly all over, basting with oil.

Put the rice on a hot serving dish and place the kebabs on
top. *Serves 4*

Crown roast

Have a crown roast prepared by the butcher, or buy two best
ends of neck. To prepare the crown yourself, cut off the chine
bone and trim the meat and fat off the tips of the bones,
leaving about 2.5 cm./1 in. of the bone exposed. Place the
two best ends back to back, forming a circle with the fat in
the middle, and tie with fine string. Put foil on the ends of the
bones to stop them scorching.

Stuff and cook as for Roast Lamb with Apricot Nut
Stuffing, using the same stuffing or a packet stuffing. If preferred, cook without stuffing and fill the centre with cooked
vegetables for serving.

Above left : Kebabs
Above right : Crown roast
Opposite : Tripe French-style (top),
Oxtail hotch-potch with mustard
dumplings (left), Fricassée of
sweetbreads (right), Kidneys
bordelaise (bottom) (recipes overleaf)

Tripe–French style

METRIC/IMPERIAL	AMERICAN
1 kg./2 lb. tripe	2 lb. tripe
30 ml./2 tablespoons oil	2 tablespoons oil
3 onions, sliced	3 onions, sliced
3 carrots, sliced	3 carrots, sliced
100 g./4 oz. mushrooms, sliced	1 cup sliced mushrooms
1 garlic clove, crushed	1 garlic clove, crushed
15 ml./1 tablespoon flour	1 tablespoon flour
300 ml./½ pint stock	1¼ cups stock
salt and pepper	salt and pepper
60 ml./4 tablespoons cream	4 tablespoons cream
30 ml./2 tablespoons brandy or sherry	2 tablespoons brandy or sherry

Cut the tripe into neat pieces and wash it in cold water. Put it in a pan, cover with cold water and bring to the boil to blanch it. Strain off the liquid and discard it.

Heat the oil in a pan and cook the vegetables and garlic for a few minutes. Stir in the flour and cook for 2 minutes. Then stir in the stock and bring it to the boil. Add the tripe and season. Lower the heat, cover the pan tightly and simmer for 40 minutes, or until tender. Mix the cream with the brandy or sherry and add it to the tripe. Cook without boiling for 5 minutes. *Serves 6*

Oxtail hotch-potch with mustard dumplings

METRIC/IMPERIAL	AMERICAN
1 good-sized oxtail, jointed	1 good-sized oxtail, jointed
3 onions, sliced	3 onions, sliced
3 large carrots, sliced	3 large carrots, sliced
1.1 l./2 pints water or brown stock	5 cups water or brown stock
grated rind of 1 lemon	grated rind of 1 lemon
bouquet garni	bouquet garni
salt and pepper	salt and pepper
40 g./1½ oz. cornflour	⅜ cup cornstarch
For the dumplings	**For the dumplings**
100 g./4 oz. self-raising flour	1 cup self-rising flour
5 ml./1 teaspoon dry mustard	1 teaspoon dry mustard
salt and pepper	salt and pepper
50 g./2 oz. shredded suet	¼ cup shredded suet
water to mix	water to mix

Put the oxtail in a large, heavy pan and fry it in its own fat until golden brown. Then lift it out of the pan and put in the onions and half the carrots. Cook them in the fat in the pan for about 5 minutes. Strain off any surplus fat, then put the oxtail back in the pan and add the water or stock, lemon rind, bouquet garni and seasoning. Simmer for 1½ hours. Then add the remaining carrot slices and simmer for 1 hour. Let the meat become quite cold, then remove the surplus fat. Reheat and add the cornflour blended with a little cold water, stirring well until the sauce thickens.

While the oxtail is cooking, make the dumplings. Sift the flour with the mustard and seasoning. Add the suet and enough water to make a soft dough. Roll into eight balls with floured hands. Bring the oxtail liquid to the boil, drop in the dumplings, then cook steadily for 20 minutes. *Serves 4 to 6*

Fricassée of sweetbreads

METRIC/IMPERIAL	AMERICAN
700 g./1½ lb. sweetbreads	1½ lb. sweetbreads
300 ml./½ pint white stock	1¼ cups white stock
1 onion	1 onion
bouquet garni	bouquet garni
thinly peeled rind of 1 lemon	thinly peeled rind of 1 lemon
little lemon juice	little lemon juice
salt and pepper	salt and pepper
25 g./1 oz. butter	2 tablespoons butter
30 ml./2 tablespoons flour	2 tablespoons flour
300 ml./½ pint milk	1¼ cups milk
15 ml./1 tablespoon chopped parsley	1 tablespoon chopped parsley
30 ml./2 tablespoons cream	2 tablespoons cream
For the garnish	**For the garnish**
3–4 slices of bread	3–4 slices of bread
50 g./2 oz. dripping or butter	¼ cup dripping or butter

Wash the sweetbreads in cold water, then put in a pan and cover with cold water. Bring the water to the boil to blanch, then drain and discard the liquid. Put the sweetbreads in a pan with the stock, whole peeled onion, bouquet garni, lemon rind and a little lemon juice. Season well and simmer gently for 30 to 35 minutes, or until the sweetbreads are tender. Strain off the stock and reserve it. Allow the sweetbreads to cool, then remove any pieces of skin.

Melt the butter in a pan, stir in the flour and cook for 2 minutes. Gradually blend in the milk, stirring constantly. Bring to the boil, then lower the heat and cook until thickened, stirring constantly. Stir about 150 ml./¼ pint (⅝ cup) of the reserved cooking liquid into the sauce. Put in the sweetbreads and heat thoroughly. Add the chopped parsley, extra seasoning if necessary and the cream.

While the sweetbreads are cooking, remove the crusts from the bread and cut the slices into triangles. Fry them in hot dripping or butter until golden brown. Place the sweetbreads in a hot serving dish and arrange the fried bread round the edge. *Serves 5 to 6*

Creamed kidneys

Kidneys bordelaise

METRIC/IMPERIAL
about 20 lambs' kidneys,
  skinned, cored and halved
40 g./1½ oz. flour
salt and pepper
pinch of grated nutmeg
50 g./2 oz. butter
2 medium onions, sliced
2 bacon rashers, cut into
  narrow strips
15 ml./1 tablespoon
  chopped parsley
300 ml./½ pint brown stock
150 ml./¼ pint red wine
675 g./1½ lb. creamed
  potatoes to serve
parsley sprigs to garnish

AMERICAN
about 20 lambs' kidneys,
  skinned, cored and
  halved
⅜ cup flour
salt and pepper
pinch of grated nutmeg
¼ cup butter
2 medium onions, sliced
2 bacon slices, cut into
  narrow strips
1 tablespoon chopped
  parsley
1¼ cups brown stock
⅝ cup red wine
3 cups creamed potatoes to
  serve
parsley sprigs to garnish

Roll the kidneys in the flour mixed with seasoning and nutmeg. Melt the butter in a large pan and fry the onions and bacon gently for a few minutes. Add the kidneys and cook gently for 5 minutes, stirring well. Add the chopped parsley, then gradually blend in the stock and wine. Bring the sauce to the boil, then lower the heat and cook until thickened, stirring constantly. Cover the pan and simmer for about 15 minutes.

    Meanwhile pipe the creamed potatoes round the edge of a serving dish and brown under the grill (broiler). Spoon the kidney mixture into the centre of the potato ring and garnish with parsley sprigs.

Serves 5 to 6

Creamed kidneys

METRIC/IMPERIAL
1 green pepper, cut into
  strips
1 red pepper, cut into strips
salt and pepper
8 lambs' kidneys, skinned,
  cored and sliced
25 g./1 oz. flour
50 g./2 oz. butter
45 ml./3 tablespoons dry
  sherry
150 ml./¼ pint single cream
175 g./6 oz. long grain rice

AMERICAN
1 green pepper, cut into
  strips
1 red pepper, cut into strips
salt and pepper
8 lambs' kidneys, skinned,
  cored and sliced
¼ cup flour
¼ cup butter
3 tablespoons dry sherry
⅝ cup light cream
1 cup long grain rice

Blanch the strips of pepper by cooking them in boiling seasoned water for 3 to 4 minutes. Then drain them. Roll the kidneys in seasoned flour. Melt the butter in a large pan and fry the peppers for a few minutes, then lift them out and keep them hot. Cook the kidneys in the pan for 8 to 10 minutes, or until tender. Turn the meat several times while cooking. Mix the sherry and cream in a bowl. Remove the pan from the heat, add the sherry and cream mixture and stir well. Return to low heat for 2 to 3 minutes and add the peppers to heat through.

    While the kidneys and peppers are being prepared, cook the rice in boiling salted water. Drain it and arrange in a ring in a hot dish. Spoon the kidneys and peppers in the centre of the ring.

Serves 3 to 4

Above : Liver sicilienne ; Above right : Kidney kebabs with orange sauce

Liver sicilienne

METRIC/IMPERIAL	AMERICAN
550 g./1¼ lb. ox liver, cut into strips	1¼ lb. ox liver, cut into strips
25 g./1 oz. flour	¼ cup flour
salt and pepper	salt and pepper
50 g./2 oz. dripping or fat	¼ cup dripping or fat
3 medium onions, sliced	3 medium onions, sliced
1 garlic clove, crushed	1 garlic clove, crushed
300 ml./½ pint stock	1¼ cups stock
300 ml./½ pint cider or red wine	1¼ cups cider or red wine
15 ml./1 tablespoon redcurrant jelly	1 tablespoon redcurrant jelly
2.5 ml./½ teaspoon grated lemon rind	½ teaspoon grated lemon rind
45 ml./3 tablespoons green olives	3 tablespoons green olives

Coat the liver with seasoned flour. Melt the dripping or fat in a pan and quickly brown the liver in it. Then lift out the liver and fry the onion rings and garlic for a few minutes. Gradually blend in the stock and cider or wine, then bring to the boil and cook until slightly thickened. Add the redcurrant jelly and lemon rind. Replace the liver, cover the pan and simmer very slowly for about 2 hours. Add the olives just before serving. Serve with creamed potatoes, boiled rice or noodles. *Serves 4 to 5*

Kidney kebabs with orange sauce

METRIC/IMPERIAL	AMERICAN
8–12 lambs' kidneys, skinned, cored and halved	8–12 lambs' kidneys, skinned, cored and halved
salt and pepper	salt and pepper
pinch of dried, mixed herbs	pinch of dried, mixed herbs
12 button mushrooms	12 button mushrooms
12 small pickling onions	12 small pickling onions
4 bacon rashers, halved	4 bacon slices, halved
50 g./2 oz. butter, melted	¼ cup melted butter
boiled rice to serve	boiled rice to serve
For the sauce	**For the sauce**
thinly peeled rind and juice of 2 oranges	thinly peeled rind and juice of 2 oranges
300 ml./½ pint brown stock	1¼ cups brown stock
25 g./1 oz. cornflour	¼ cup cornstarch
25 g./1 oz. butter	2 tablespoons butter
salt and pepper	salt and pepper
2.5 ml./½ teaspoon sugar	½ teaspoon sugar

Roll the kidneys in seasoning and herbs. Put them on skewers with the mushrooms, onions and rolled bacon, alternating them. Brush with the melted butter and cook under a hot grill (broiler) for about 8 minutes. Turn several times during cooking so that the food cooks evenly.

To make the sauce, simmer the rind in half the stock for about 5 minutes. Then strain the stock and return it to the pan. Mix the cornflour (cornstarch) with the rest of the stock and add it to the pan with the orange juice, the butter, seasoning and sugar. Stir well and bring the sauce to the boil. Then lower the heat and cook gently until the sauce is smooth and thickened, stirring constantly. Segments of orange may be added, if wished. Serve the kebabs on a bed of boiled rice, with the sauce. *Serves 4*

Kidneys with spring onions (scallions) and cauliflower

Kidneys with
spring onions (scallions) and cauliflower

METRIC/IMPERIAL

4 lambs' kidneys, cored and
  sliced
30 ml./2 tablespoons sherry
1 small cauliflower, in
  florets
30 ml./2 tablespoons oil
4 spring onions, cut into
  2.5 cm./1 in. lengths
15 ml./1 tablespoon
  cornflour
15 ml./1 tablespoon soy
  sauce
5 ml./1 teaspoon brown
  sugar
5 ml./1 teaspoon salt

AMERICAN

4 lambs' kidneys, cored and
  sliced
2 tablespoons sherry
1 small cauliflower, in
  florets
2 tablespoons oil
4 scallions, cut into 1 in.
  lengths
1 tablespoon cornstarch
1 tablespoon soy sauce
1 teaspoon brown sugar
1 teaspoon salt

Soak the kidneys in the sherry. Cook the cauliflower in boiling salted water for 3 minutes, then drain. Melt the oil in a frying pan and fry the drained kidneys and cauliflower with the spring onions (scallions) for 2 minutes. Mix the cornflour (cornstarch) to a smooth paste with the soy sauce, 30 ml./2 tablespoons water, the sugar, the remaining sherry and the salt. Add to the pan and cook gently for 3 minutes, stirring constantly. Serve with boiled rice. *Serves 3 to 4*

Liver and spring onions (scallions)

METRIC/IMPERIAL
½ kg./1 lb. liver, cut in
small slices
15 ml./1 tablespoon
cornflour
30 ml./2 tablespoons sherry
30 ml./2 tablespoons soy
sauce
30 ml./2 tablespoons oil
2 spring onions, chopped
2 leeks, thickly sliced
5 ml./1 teaspoon brown
sugar
pinch of salt

AMERICAN
1 lb. liver, cut in small
slices
1 tablespoon cornstarch
2 tablespoons sherry
2 tablespoons soy sauce
2 tablespoons oil
2 scallions, chopped
2 leeks, thickly sliced
1 teaspoon brown sugar
pinch of salt

Cover the liver with boiling water and leave for 1 minute, then drain. Mix the cornflour (cornstarch), sherry and soy sauce to a smooth paste, add it to the liver and mix well. Heat the oil in a frying pan and fry the liver for 1 minute over fierce heat, stirring constantly. Add the spring onions (scallions), leeks, sugar, salt and any remaining cornflour (cornstarch) mixture. Heat quickly, stirring, for 1 minute. Serve with boiled rice. *Serves 4*

Lemon garlic kidneys

METRIC/IMPERIAL
12 lambs' kidneys, skinned, cored and sliced
salt and pepper
1 garlic clove, chopped
30 ml./2 tablespoons olive oil
juice of 1 lemon
boiled rice to serve
lemon wedges to garnish

AMERICAN
12 lambs' kidneys, skinned, cored and sliced
salt and pepper
1 garlic clove, chopped
2 tablespoons olive oil
juice of 1 lemon
boiled rice to serve
lemon wedges to garnish

Season the kidneys and fry them with the garlic in hot oil for 3 to 4 minutes, turning them constantly. Squeeze the lemon juice over the kidneys and remove from the heat. Serve on a bed of boiled rice and garnish with lemon. *Serves 4*

Braised liver with mushrooms and rice

METRIC/IMPERIAL
25 g./1 oz. butter
½ small onion, grated
15 ml./1 tablespoon flour
1.25 ml./¼ teaspoon salt
pinch of pepper
225 g./8 oz. liver, chopped
225 g./8 oz. mushrooms, sliced
150 ml./¼ pint stock
175 g./6 oz. rice
For garnish
parsley sprigs
paprika

AMERICAN
2 tablespoons butter
½ small onion, grated
1 tablespoon flour
¼ teaspoon salt
pinch of pepper
8 oz. liver, chopped
2 cups sliced mushrooms
⅝ cup stock
1 cup rice
For garnish
parsley sprigs
paprika

Melt the butter in a pan and cook the onion gently until soft. Mix the flour, salt and pepper and coat the pieces of liver in it. Add the liver to the pan and fry gently with the onion. Add the mushrooms and cook for a few minutes. Then add the stock and bring to the boil. Place the contents of the pan in an ovenproof casserole and cover tightly. Cook in the oven preheated to warm (170°C/325°F or Gas Mark 3) for 45 minutes.

Meanwhile cook the rice in plenty of boiling salted water until tender but not mushy. Strain the rice and rinse in hot water, then press it into a greased ring pan. Press the rice down tightly, then turn it on to a hot dish. Put the cooked liver mixture in the centre of the rice ring. Garnish with parsley and sprinkle over paprika. *Serves 3*

Opposite : Liver and spring onions (scallions)
Above right : Lemon garlic kidneys
Right : Braised liver with mushrooms and rice

Poultry & game

Chicken with white wine and mushrooms

Chicken with white wine and mushrooms

METRIC/IMPERIAL
1 chicken, about 1½ kg./3 lb.
50 g./2 oz. butter
12 small onions or shallots
100 g./4 oz. bacon, diced
15 g./½ oz. flour
100 g./4 oz. button
  mushrooms
150 ml./¼ pint white wine
150 ml./¼ pint chicken stock
bouquet garni
salt and freshly ground
  black pepper

AMERICAN
1 chicken, about 3 lb.
¼ cup butter
12 small onions or shallots
4 oz. bacon, diced
2 tablespoons flour
1 cup button mushrooms
⅝ cup white wine
⅝ cup chicken stock
bouquet garni
salt and freshly ground
  black pepper

Cut the chicken into four portions. Melt the butter in a large pan and fry the chicken pieces until they are brown all over. Remove the chicken pieces from the pan and drain on absorbent paper. Put the onions or shallots and bacon in the pan and fry until softened. Add the flour and cook, stirring, for 2 to 3 minutes. Then add the mushrooms, wine, stock, bouquet garni, salt and pepper. Bring to the boil, then lower the heat, return the chicken, cover, and simmer for 35 to 45 minutes, or until the chicken is tender.

Remove the bouquet garni. Serve the chicken in a heated dish with the sauce poured over it. *Serves 4*

Chicken cacciatore

Chicken cacciatore

METRIC/IMPERIAL
1 chicken, 1½–2 kg./
    3–4 lb.
flour
50 g./2 oz. butter
15 ml./1 tablespoon olive
    oil
1 large onion, chopped
2 garlic cloves, chopped
8 tomatoes, skinned and
    chopped
45 ml./3 tablespoons
    tomato purée
5 ml./1 teaspoon sugar
150 ml./¼ pint chicken stock
salt and pepper
225 g./8 oz. button
    mushrooms, sliced
60 ml./4 tablespoons
    Marsala wine

AMERICAN
1 chicken, 3–4 lb.
flour
¼ cup butter
1 tablespoon olive oil
1 large onion, chopped
2 garlic cloves, chopped
8 tomatoes, skinned and
    chopped
3 tablespoons tomato purée
1 teaspoon sugar
⅝ cup chicken stock
salt and pepper
2 cups sliced button
    mushrooms
4 tablespoons Marsala wine

Cut the chicken into joints and coat them with flour. Heat the butter and olive oil together in a large pan. Add the chicken joints and fry until crisp and golden all over. Remove from the pan and keep hot. Add the onion and garlic to the pan and fry gently until pale gold. Stir in the tomatoes, tomato purée, sugar and stock, then season well with salt and pepper. Bring to the boil, then replace the chicken. Reduce the heat, cover the pan and simmer slowly for 30 to 45 minutes. Add the mushrooms and Marsala and continue to cook for 10 to 15 minutes. Serve with pasta. *Serves 4*

Chicken in wine Italian-style

METRIC/IMPERIAL
1 chicken, about 2 kg./4 lb.
flour
salt and pepper
50 g./2 oz. butter
60 ml./4 tablespoons olive
   oil
1 medium onion, chopped
2 medium carrots, thinly
   sliced
2 celery stalks, thinly sliced
chicken liver, chopped
150 ml./¼ pint chicken stock
150 ml./¼ pint dry red wine
5 ml./1 teaspoon dried basil
100 g./4 oz. mushrooms,
   sliced
10 ml./2 teaspoons finely
   chopped parsley
45 ml./3 tablespoons
   Marsala wine
watercress to garnish

AMERICAN
1 chicken, about 4 lb.
flour
salt and pepper
¼ cup butter
4 tablespoons olive oil
1 medium onion, chopped
2 medium carrots, thinly
   sliced
2 celery stalks, thinly sliced
chicken liver, chopped
⅝ cup chicken stock
⅝ cup dry red wine
1 teaspoon dried basil
1 cup sliced mushrooms
2 teaspoons finely chopped
   parsley
3 tablespoons Marsala wine
watercress to garnish

Cut the chicken into joints and sprinkle them with flour mixed with a little salt and pepper. Heat the butter and olive oil together in a large pan. Add the chicken and fry until golden-brown all over. Remove the joints from the pan and keep them hot. Add the onion, carrots, celery and chicken liver to the butter and oil remaining in the pan and cook slowly until the onion is golden. Add the stock, wine, basil and mushrooms, then replace the chicken joints. Cover and cook gently for 30 minutes. Then add seasoning, parsley and Marsala and continue to simmer until the chicken is tender. Garnish with watercress. Serve with pasta or buttered new potatoes and a green salad.

Serves 4

Above : Chicken in wine Italian-style
Opposite top : Old English chicken pie
Opposite bottom : Chicken and pear vol-au-vents

Chicken and pear vol-au-vents

METRIC/IMPERIAL	AMERICAN
225 g./8 oz. quantity puff pastry	2 cup quantity puff pastry
1 egg, beaten	1 egg, beaten
225 g./8 oz. cold cooked chicken	2 cups cold cooked chicken
300 ml./½ pint béchamel sauce	1¼ cups béchamel sauce
1 egg yolk	1 egg yolk
juice of ½ lemon	juice of ½ lemon
½ kg./1 lb. pears	1 lb. pears
1.25 ml./¼ teaspoon grated nutmeg	¼ teaspoon grated nutmeg
salt and pepper	salt and pepper

Roll out the dough on a lightly floured board to 1.25 cm./ ½ in. thick. Cut it into four rounds about 5 cm./2 in. in diameter. Mark a circle in the centre of each round, using a smaller cutter, but cut only halfway through the pastry. Mark a criss-cross pattern in the centre circle with a knife. Leave the pastry in a cool place for 20 minutes before baking. Brush the tops with beaten egg, then bake in the oven preheated to hot (240°C/475°F or Gas Mark 8) for 10 minutes. Then reduce the temperature to fairly hot (190°C/375°F or Gas Mark 5) for a further 10 to 15 minutes, or until cooked.

Meanwhile cut the chicken into bite-sized pieces. Add the egg yolk to the béchamel sauce and reheat without boiling. Stir in the chicken and lemon juice. Peel, core and chop the pears and add them to the sauce. Reheat and season with nutmet, salt and pepper.

Remove the centre circle from each vol-au-vent case, taking care not to break it. Scoop out the pastry in the middle and spoon in the sauce. Replace the lid. Serve immediately.

Serves 4

Old English chicken pie

METRIC/IMPERIAL	AMERICAN
½ packet sage and onion stuffing	½ packet sage and onion stuffing
350 g./12 oz. diced raw chicken	2 cups diced raw chicken
50 g./2 oz. flour	½ cup flour
salt and pepper	salt and pepper
3 skinless sausages	3 skinless sausages
50 g./2 oz. butter	¼ cup butter
400 ml./¾ pint chicken stock	2 cups chicken stock
2 eggs, hardboiled and chopped	2 eggs, hardcooked and chopped
225 g./8 oz. quantity shortcrust pastry	2 cup quantity shortcrust pastry
1 egg to glaze	1 egg to glaze

Make up the stuffing and form it into small balls. Toss the chicken in half the flour mixed with a little seasoning. Cut the sausages in half. Melt the butter in a pan and brown the stuffing balls, chicken and sausages. Then remove them from the pan and put in a pie dish of about 1¼ l./2 pints (5 cups) capacity. Stir the remaining flour into any fat remaining in the pan, cook for 2 minutes, then gradually stir in the stock. Bring to the boil and cook until thickened, stirring constantly. Add the hardboiled eggs to the sauce and pour it over the chicken, sausages and stuffing balls. Allow to cool slightly.

Roll out the dough to 6 mm./¼ in. thickness to cover the pie dish. From the trimmings, make a strip of dough to go round the moistened edge of the pie dish. Brush the rim of dough with a little water. Place the dough lid over the pie dish, using a rolling pin to ease it over. Press the edges together, cut away any surplus and flute the edge with a knife. Cut a slit in the top and decorate with dough leaves made from the trimmings.

Bake in the centre of the oven preheated to hot (220°C/ 425°F or Gas Mark 7) for about 20 minutes or until the pastry is golden brown. Then reduce the heat to moderate (180°C/ 350°F or Gas Mark 4) and bake for a further 20 minutes. Serve hot.

Serves 6

Fried chicken with green peppers

METRIC/IMPERIAL	AMERICAN
2 poussins (baby spring chickens)	2 poussins (baby spring chickens)
garlic clove	garlic clove
juice of $\frac{1}{2}$ lemon	juice of $\frac{1}{2}$ lemon
flour	flour
salt and pepper	salt and pepper
50 g./2 oz. butter	$\frac{1}{4}$ cup butter
60 ml./4 tablespoons olive oil	4 tablespoons olive oil
1 onion, sliced	1 onion, sliced
1 green pepper, coarsely chopped	1 green pepper, coarsely chopped
2.5 ml./$\frac{1}{2}$ teaspoon dried rosemary	$\frac{1}{2}$ teaspoon dried rosemary
60 ml./4 tablespoons Marsala wine	4 tablespoons Marsala wine
lemon slices to garnish	lemon slices to garnish

Cut each chicken into halves or quarters, depending on size. Rub them with a cut garlic clove and sprinkle with lemon juice. Dust the joints lightly with well-seasoned flour.

Heat the butter and olive oil together in a large frying pan. Add the pieces of chicken, skin side up, and fry until golden, then turn and fry the other side. Remove the chicken from the pan and keep it hot. Fry the onion and green pepper in the butter and oil remaining in the pan. After a few minutes, add the rosemary and Marsala. Then return the chicken joints to the pan, cover, and continue to cook until the chicken is tender. Garnish with lemon slices. *Serves 4*

Terrine of chicken

METRIC/IMPERIAL	AMERICAN
1 roasting chicken, about 1¾ kg./3½ lb.	1 roasting chicken, about 3½ lb.
225 g./8 oz. lean pork or veal	8 oz. lean pork or veal
350 g./12 oz. thin bacon rashers	12 oz. thin bacon slices
salt and pepper	salt and pepper
225 g./8 oz. pork sausage meat	8 oz. pork sausage meat
60 ml./4 tablespoons strong chicken stock, made from the giblets	4 tablespoons strong chicken stock, made from the giblets
15 ml./1 tablespoon chopped parsley	1 tablespoon chopped parsley

Remove the skin from the chicken and cut the breast meat into neat slices. Remove the rest of the chicken meat from the bones and mince (grind) it with the pork or veal and two bacon rashers (slices). Season the minced (ground) meat well and mix it with the sausage meat and half the stock.

Line the bottom of an oval or oblong ovenproof dish with half the remaining bacon rashers (slices). Put a layer of the minced (ground) meat over the slices. Then add some of the sliced chicken breast, sprinkle it lightly with stock and chopped parsley. Continue filling the dish like this, ending with minced (ground) meat. Cover with the remaining bacon rashers (slices). Cover with a well-fitting lid or foil.

Stand the dish in a roasting pan of cold water and cook in the centre of the oven preheated to warm (170°C/325°F or Gas Mark 3) for 1½ hours. Remove the lid or foil and put a light weight (about 1 kg./2 lb.) over the terrine so that it is pressed into a neat shape as it cools. Turn out when cold.

Serves 4 to 6

Opposite top : Fried chicken with green peppers
Opposite bottom : Chicken in red wine
Above : Terrine of chicken

Chicken in red wine

METRIC/IMPERIAL	AMERICAN
1 chicken, about 1½ kg./3 lb.	1 chicken, about 3 lb.
75 g./3 oz. butter	6 tablespoons butter
8 small onions or shallots	8 small onions or shallots
4 rashers streaky bacon, diced	4 slices streaky bacon, diced
45 ml./3 tablespoons brandy	3 tablespoons brandy
300 ml./½ pint chicken stock	1¼ cups chicken stock
salt and freshly ground black pepper	salt and freshly ground black pepper
bouquet garni	bouquet garni
2 garlic cloves, crushed	2 garlic cloves, crushed
100 g./4 oz. button mushrooms	1 cup button mushrooms
25 g./1 oz. flour	¼ cup flour

For the garnish

chopped parsley	chopped parsley
croûtes of fried bread	croûtes of fried bread

For the garnish

Cut the chicken into four portions. Melt 50 g./2 oz. (4 table-spoons) of the butter in a large pan and fry the chicken until golden, then remove it and drain on absorbent paper. Then fry the onions and bacon in the pan until golden, stirring occasionally. Return the chicken to the pan, pour in the brandy and set light to it. When the flames have died down add the stock, salt, pepper, bouquet garni, garlic and mushrooms. Bring to the boil, then reduce the heat, cover and simmer for 35 to 45 minutes or until the chicken is tender.

Remove the chicken joints from the pan and discard the bouquet garni. Place the chicken on a heated serving dish and keep hot. Mix the remaining butter with the flour to a smooth paste. Bring the cooking liquid to the boil and add the butter and flour mixture in small pieces, stirring constantly, until the sauce has thickened. Allow the sauce to boil for 2 to 3 minutes.

Pour the sauce over the chicken, sprinkle with chopped parsley and arrange the croûtes around the edge of the dish. Serve very hot.

Serves 4

Dry chicken curry with yellow rice

METRIC/IMPERIAL
40 g./1½ oz. butter
1 large onion, chopped
1 green pepper, sliced
1 garlic clove, crushed
15 ml./1 tablespoon Madras
   curry powder
5 ml./1 teaspoon chilli
   powder
salt
4 chicken joints
4 tomatoes
30 ml./2 tablespoons yogurt
For the rice
25 g./1 oz. butter
225 g./8 oz. long grain rice
5 ml./1 teaspoon turmeric
few cloves
5 ml./1 teaspoon ground
   cumin
salt
600 ml./1 pint water

AMERICAN
3 tablespoons butter
1 large onion, chopped
1 green pepper, sliced
1 garlic clove, crushed
1 tablespoon Madras
   curry powder
1 teaspoon chili powder
salt
4 chicken joints
4 tomatoes
2 tablespoons yogurt
For the rice
2 tablespoons butter
1⅓ cups long grain rice
1 teaspoon turmeric
few cloves
1 teaspoon ground cumin
salt
2½ cups water

Melt the butter in a pan and fry the onion, pepper and garlic for about 5 minutes. Add the curry powder, chilli powder and a pinch of salt; mix well. Put the chicken joints in the pan and brown quickly over high heat. Then lower the heat, cover and simmer gently for 1 hour. If the chicken joints are fresh, add 2 to 3 tablespoons of water before lowering the heat: frozen chicken will probably not need water. Add the whole tomatoes to the pan 5 minutes before the end of the cooking time. Stir in the yogurt just before serving.

While the chicken is cooking, prepare the rice. Heat the butter in a pan and toss the rice in it for 5 minutes. Add the spices and a pinch of salt and mix well. Pour in the water, bring to the boil, then cover and simmer gently for 15 minutes or until the rice is tender and all the liquid absorbed. If wished, the rice can be garnished with a few thin strips of cucumber.

The curry may be served with sliced onion, peanuts and poppadums. *Serves 4*

*Opposite : Dry chicken curry with
yellow rice*
Right : Fried chicken Italienne

Fried chicken Italienne

METRIC/IMPERIAL	AMERICAN
8 chicken drumsticks	8 chicken drumsticks
15 ml./1 tablespoon flour	1 tablespoon flour
salt and pepper	salt and pepper
1 large egg, beaten	1 large egg, beaten
75 g./3 oz. dry bread-crumbs	1 cup dry breadcrumbs
30 ml./2 tablespoons grated Parmesan cheese	2 tablespoons grated Parmesan cheese
deep fat or oil for frying	deep fat or oil for frying
watercress to garnish	watercress to garnish
For the rice mixture	**For the rice mixture**
50 g./2 oz. butter	¼ cup butter
1 green pepper, diced	1 green pepper, diced
1 red pepper, diced	1 red pepper, diced
225 g./8 oz. long grain rice	1⅓ cup long grain rice
600 ml./1 pint chicken stock	2½ cups chicken stock
salt and pepper	salt and pepper
100 g./4 oz. cooked peas	1 cup cooked peas
75 g./3 oz. canned sweetcorn, drained	½ cup canned sweetcorn, drained

Coat the drumsticks with seasoned flour, then with beaten egg and finally with the crumbs mixed with the grated cheese. If possible, chill for a while so that the coating sets.

Melt the butter in a pan and cook the peppers for a few minutes. Add the rice and stir it in the butter until the grains are transparent. Add the stock and bring to the boil, stirring. Season well and cook until the rice is nearly tender, then add the peas and sweetcorn. Continue cooking until the rice is tender and the liquid is absorbed.

Meanwhile deep fry the chicken drumsticks in hot fat or oil. Take care that the fat or oil is not too hot, otherwise the cheese will scorch. Drain the drumsticks on absorbent paper. Pile the rice mixture onto a hot dish and arrange the drumsticks round it. Garnish with sprigs of watercress. *Serves 4*

Roast stuffed duck with orange sauce

METRIC/IMPERIAL	AMERICAN
1 duck (1–1½ kg./4–5 lb.)	1 duck (4–5 lb.)
salt and pepper	salt and pepper
garlic clove (optional)	garlic clove (optional)
juice of 1 orange	juice of 1 orange
For the stuffing	**For the stuffing**
25 g./1 oz. chicken fat	2 tablespoons chicken fat
1 small onion, chopped	1 small onion, chopped
50 g./2 oz. raisins, soaked in 2 tablespoons hot stock	⅓ cup raisins, soaked in 2 tablespoons hot stock
225 g./8 oz. long grain rice, cooked	4 cups cooked long grain rice
1 apple, peeled and chopped	1 apple, peeled and chopped
salt	salt
For the orange sauce	**For the orange sauce**
15 ml./1 tablespoon flour	1 tablespoon flour
juice and rind of 1 orange	juice and rind of 1 orange
juice and rind of ½ lemon	juice and rind of ½ lemon
150 ml./¼ pint stock	⅝ cup stock
salt and pepper	salt and pepper

Melt the fat for the stuffing in a pan and fry the onion. Mix in the raisins, rice, apple and seasoning.

Season the duck with salt and pepper and rub the outside with the cut clove of garlic. Stuff the bird and place it on a rack in a roasting pan. Pour the orange juice over and cover the breast with foil. Cook in the oven preheated to hot (220°C/425°F or Gas Mark 7). After 15 minutes, turn the oven down to fairly hot (190°C/375°F or Gas Mark 5). Remove the foil 30 minutes before the end of the cooking time (1½–2 hours, according to size).

Remove the duck from the oven and keep it hot. Pour off the fat except for 15 ml./1 tablespoon. Add the flour for the sauce and cook until brown. Add the juice and rind of 1 orange and ½ lemon and the stock. Cook until thick, stirring continually. Adjust seasoning and strain the sauce into a gravy boat. *Serves 5 to 6*

Note: Stock can be made by boiling the giblets, onion and seasoning.

Roast duck with Marsala

METRIC/IMPERIAL
2 fresh sage leaves, or
   1.25 ml./¼ teaspoon dried
   sage
1 garlic clove, halved
1 duck (about 2 kg./4 lb.)
salt and pepper
75 ml./5 tablespoons
   Marsala

AMERICAN
2 fresh sage leaves, or
   ¼ teaspoon dried sage
1 garlic clove, halved
1 duck (about 4 lb.)
salt and pepper
5 tablespoons Marsala

Put the sage and garlic in the body cavity of the duck and place it on a rack in a large roasting pan. Prick the skin all over with a fork, then sprinkle with salt and pepper. Pour the Marsala into the pan. Roast in the centre of the oven pre-heated to fairly hot (190°C/375°F or Gas Mark 5) for 1½ hours, basting at least twice.

Serves 4

Casserole of duck

METRIC/IMPERIAL	AMERICAN
1 large duck	1 large duck
12 very small onions	12 very small onions
1 garlic clove, crushed	1 garlic clove, crushed
4 carrots, halved or quartered	4 carrots, halved or quartered
400 ml./¾ pint duck stock (made from the giblets)	2 cups duck stock (made from the giblets)
salt and pepper	salt and pepper
25 g./1 oz. flour	¼ cup flour
4 large potatoes, sliced	4 large potatoes, sliced
parsley sprig to garnish	parsley sprig to garnish
For the sage and onion stuffing	**For the sage and onion stuffing**
2 large onions, chopped	2 large onions, chopped
150 ml./¼ pint water	⅝ cup water
salt and pepper	salt and pepper
75 g./3 oz. soft white breadcrumbs	1 cup soft white breadcrumbs
5–10 ml./1–2 teaspoons chopped fresh sage, or 2.5 ml./½ teaspoon dried sage	1–2 teaspoons chopped fresh sage, or ½ teaspoon dried sage
50 g./2 oz. shredded suet or melted margarine	¼ cup shredded suet or melted margarine
1 egg (optional)	1 egg (optional)

First make the stuffing. Cook the onions for 10 minutes in the water and season well. Strain, then blend the onion with the breadcrumbs, sage and suet (or margarine). Bind with the onion liquid or an egg. Place the stuffing in the cavity of the duck and roast in the oven preheated to hot (220–230°C/425–450°F or Gas Mark 7–8) for about 30 minutes, or until the skin is crisp and brown and much of the fat has run out.

While the duck is cooking, simmer the onions, garlic and carrots in 300 ml./½ pint (1¼ cups) of the stock for 30 minutes; season well. Blend the flour with the remaining stock, stir it into the vegetables and cook until there is a smooth, thickened sauce. Transfer the vegetables and sauce to an ovenproof casserole and put in the sliced potatoes. Place the duck on top, cover, and cook for 1½ hours in the centre of the oven preheated to moderate (180°C/350°F or Gas Mark 4). Garnish with parsley. *Serves 4*

Creamed turkey duchesse

METRIC/IMPERIAL	AMERICAN
450 g./1 lb. mashed potatoes	2 cups mashed potatoes
2 eggs or 2 egg yolks	2 eggs or 2 egg yolks
2 oz. butter	¼ cup butter
salt and pepper	salt and pepper
100 g./4 oz. button mushrooms	1 cup button mushrooms
1 green pepper, seeded and diced	1 green pepper, seeded and diced
300 ml./½ pint stock (made from turkey carcass or giblets)	1¼ cups stock (made from turkey carcass or giblets)
25 g./1 oz. flour	¼ cup flour
150 ml./¼ pint milk	⅝ cup milk
few drops of Tabasco sauce	few drops of Tabasco sauce
450 g./1 lb. diced cooked turkey	1 lb. diced cooked turkey
30–45 ml./2–3 tablespoons single cream	2–3 tablespoons light cream
chopped parsley to garnish	chopped parsley to garnish

Mix the mashed potatoes with 1 egg or egg yolk and half the butter; season well. Form the potato into a border round an ovenproof dish. Brush with the second egg or egg yolk, diluted with a few drops of water, and brown in the oven preheated to moderate (180°C/350°F or Gas Mark 4).

Meanwhile simmer the whole mushrooms and diced green pepper in the stock for 10 minutes. Strain off the liquid and put it aside for the sauce.

Heat the remainder of the butter in a pan, stir in the flour and cook for 2 minutes, stirring. Gradually stir in the milk, then the stock. Bring to the boil and cook until the sauce thickens, stirring constantly. Season well and flavour with Tabasco. Put the vegetables and turkey in the sauce and heat gently for a few minutes. Stir in the cream. Put the turkey mixture inside the potato border and garnish with parsley. *Serves 4 to 6*

Opposite top left: Roast stuffed duck with orange sauce (recipe on previous page)
Opposite top right: Casserole of duck
Opposite bottom: Roast duck with Marsala
Above right: Creamed turkey duchesse

Roast turkey with forcemeat stuffing

METRIC/IMPERIAL	AMERICAN
1 turkey	1 turkey
several rashers fat bacon, or enough bacon fat to cover the bird	several slices fat bacon, or enough bacon fat to cover the bird
For the stuffing	**For the stuffing**
125 g./4 oz. lean ham, chopped	4 oz. lean ham, chopped
225 g./8 oz. sausage meat	8 oz. sausage meat
5 ml./1 teaspoon chopped parsley	1 teaspoon chopped parsley
grated rind of 1 lemon	grated rind of 1 lemon
50 g./2 oz. sultanas	⅓ cup golden raisins
1 egg, beaten	1 egg, beaten
salt and pepper	salt and pepper
For the garnish	**For the garnish**
225 g./8 oz. streaky bacon rashers	8 oz. streaky bacon slices
½ kg./1 lb. small sausages	1 lb. small sausages
watercress sprig	watercress sprig
For the gravy	**For the gravy**
15–30 ml./1–2 tablespoons flour	1–2 tablespoons flour
300–600 ml./½–1 pint stock (made from the giblets)	1¼–2½ cups stock (made from the giblets)

Roast turkey with forcemeat stuffing

Combine all the ingredients for the stuffing and season well. Lift the skin of the neck of the turkey and place stuffing under it. Pull the skin gently over the stuffing and fasten it with a skewer. Put any remaining stuffing inside the bird. Cross the legs over the vent and secure them with string. Weigh the bird to calculate the cooking time (see below). Cover the bird with the bacon or bacon fat, making sure the breast is well covered. Place the turkey in a roasting pan and cook in the preheated oven: baste from time to time to keep the flesh moist. Set the oven at hot (220–230°C/425–450°F or Gas Mark 7–8) and reduce the heat after 30 minutes to moderate (180–190°C/350–375°F or Gas Mark 4–5). Allow 15 minutes per ½ kg./1 lb. and 15 minutes over for a bird up to 6 kg./12 lb. in weight. After that, add 12 minutes per ½ kg./1 lb. up to 10½ kg./21 lb.: above that weight, allow only 10 more minutes for each additional ½ kg./1 lb. If the bird is exceptionally broad breasted, allow a little extra time.

To make the garnish, remove the bacon rind and cut the rashers (slices) in half. Stretch each slice with the blunt edge of a knife, then roll up and secure with a wooden or metal skewer. Grill (broil) the bacon rolls and sausages and place round the cooked turkey. Garnish with watercress. Make the gravy with the flour, stock and juices in the roasting pan. Serve with cranberry sauce.

A 6 kg./12 lb. turkey serves 14 to 16

Roast pheasants

METRIC/IMPERIAL	AMERICAN
50 g./2 oz. butter, or bacon fat	¼ cup butter, or bacon fat
2 young pheasants	2 young pheasants
2 rashers fat bacon	2 slices fat bacon
salt and pepper	salt and pepper
For the gravy	**For the gravy**
1 tablespoon flour	1 tablespoon flour
300 ml./½ pint stock (made from the giblets)	1¼ cups stock (made from the giblets)

Place a small knob of butter or bacon fat inside each bird and truss. Melt the rest of the butter or fat in a roasting pan, place the birds in the pan and spoon the butter over them. Lay the bacon over the top of the birds. Put them in the oven preheated to hot (220–230°C/425–450°F or Gas Mark 7–8) and roast for 15 minutes or until tender. Lower the heat to moderate (180–190°C/350–375°F or Gas Mark 4–5) and roast for a further 30 to 35 minutes. Baste from time to time to keep the birds moist.

To make the gravy, pour off the fat from the roasting pan. Mix the flour with the juices left in the pan and cook for 2 minutes. Then stir in the stock, bring to the boil and cook until thickened, stirring well. Add a little salt and pepper and strain the gravy.

Serve garnished with button mushrooms cooked in butter, if wished. Traditional accompaniments for pheasant are fried crumbs, bread sauce and game chips. *Serves 8*

Above : Roast goose ; Below : Roast pheasants

Roast goose

METRIC/IMPERIAL	AMERICAN
1 goose	1 goose
15 ml./1 tablespoon flour	1 tablespoon flour
300 ml./½ pint stock, made from the giblets	1¼ cups stock, made from the giblets
For sage and onion stuffing	**For sage and onion stuffing**
2 large onions, chopped	2 large onions, chopped
150 ml./¼ pint water	⅝ cup water
salt and pepper	salt and pepper
75 g./3 oz. fresh white breadcrumbs	1 cup fresh white breadcrumbs
5 ml./1 teaspoon chopped fresh sage, or 2.5 ml./½ teaspoon dried sage	1 teaspoon chopped fresh sage, or ½ teaspoon dried sage
50 g./2 oz. shredded suet or melted margarine	¼ cup shredded suet or melted margarine
1 egg, beaten	1 egg, beaten

As goose is very fatty, no extra fat is needed for cooking: place the bird on a rack in the roasting pan to allow the fat to drain off. To make the stuffing, cook the onions in the water for 10 minutes, then strain them and season well. Keep a little of the water for the stuffing. Combine all the ingredients, using just enough egg to bind the stuffing and moisten with a little of the onion water. Place the stuffing inside the goose and truss. Roast in the oven preheated to hot (220–230°C/ 425–450°F or Gas Mark 7–8). After 30 minutes reduce the heat to moderate (180°C/350°F or Gas Mark 4). Allow 15 minutes per ½ kg./1 lb. and 15 minutes over. Prick the goose all over with a fork two or three times during cooking to allow the fat to run.

Make gravy with the flour, juices in the pan and the stock. Serve with apple sauce.

A goose weighing 6 kg./12 lb. serves about 8

Hare in Madeira sauce

METRIC/IMPERIAL
saddle joints of 1 young
   hare
15 ml./1 tablespoon flour
2.5 ml./½ teaspoon chopped
   sage
75 g./3 oz. butter
100 g./4 oz. button
   mushrooms
200 ml./8 fl. oz. Madeira
   wine
2.5 ml./½ teaspoon chopped
   fresh herbs, or good
   pinch of dried herbs
salt and pepper

AMERICAN
saddle joints of 1 young
   hare
1 tablespoon flour
½ teaspoon chopped sage
⅜ cup butter
1 cup button mushrooms
1 cup Madeira wine
½ teaspoon chopped fresh
   herbs, or good pinch of
   dried herbs
salt and pepper

Sprinkle the hare joints with the flour mixed with the sage. Melt half the butter in a pan and fry the hare until brown. Lift the joints out of the pan and put them in an ovenproof casserole. Heat the rest of the butter and cook the mushrooms in it. Add the mushrooms to the casserole with the wine, herbs and seasoning. Cover the casserole and cook in the oven preheated to fairly hot (190–200°C/375–400°F or Gas Mark 5–6) for 1 hour. *Serves 4*

Above : Hare in Madeira sauce
Opposite : Jugged hare Landès-style

Jugged hare Landès-style

METRIC/IMPERIAL
1 hare
50 g./2 oz. pork fat
10 shallots
2 garlic cloves, crushed
100 g./4 oz. Bayonne ham
   or gammon, diced
150 ml./¼ pint red wine
300 ml./½ pint water
4 tomatoes, skinned, seeded
   and chopped
50 g./2 oz. button
   mushrooms
salt and freshly ground
   black pepper
croûtes of fried bread for
   garnish

AMERICAN
1 hare
¼ cup pork fat
10 shallots
2 garlic cloves, crushed
4 oz. Bayonne ham, diced
⅝ cup red wine
1¼ cups water
4 tomatoes, skinned, seeded
   and chopped
½ cup button mushrooms
salt and freshly ground
   black pepper
croûtes of fried bread for
   garnish

Cut the hare into serving portions. Heat the pork fat in a large pan and fry the hare until browned all over. Remove the hare, drain it on absorbent paper and place it in an ovenproof casserole. Brown the shallots in the pork fat and add them to the casserole with the remaining ingredients.

Cover the casserole tightly and cook in the oven preheated to warm (170°C/325°F or Gas Mark 3) for 1½ to 2 hours, or until the hare is very tender. Place the hare on a heated serving dish. Strain the sauce into a pan, bring to the boil and boil rapidly until it has thickened slightly. If you have some of the hare's blood, add a little to the sauce to thicken it.

Pour the sauce over the hare and garnish with croûtes of fried bread, arranged round the edge of the dish.   *Serves 6*

Dishes without meat

Cauliflower surprise

METRIC/IMPERIAL	AMERICAN
100 g./4 oz. butter	½ cup butter
2 medium onions, sliced	2 medium onions, sliced
2 tomatoes, skinned and sliced	2 tomatoes, skinned and sliced
6 mushrooms, sliced	6 mushrooms, sliced
1 small can sweetcorn, drained	1 small can sweetcorn, drained
few cooked or canned peas	few cooked or canned peas
1 medium cauliflower	1 medium cauliflower
salt and pepper	salt and pepper
50 g./2 oz. flour	½ cup flour
400 ml./¾ pint milk	2 cups milk
100 g./4 oz. cheese, grated	1 cup grated cheese

Melt half the butter in a pan and cook the onions, tomatoes and mushrooms until tender. Add the sweetcorn and peas. Heat gently and keep hot. Meanwhile cook the whole cauliflower in boiling salted water until just tender.

Melt the remaining butter in a pan, stir in the flour and cook for 2 minutes. Gradually blend in the milk and 150 ml./¼ pint (⅔ cup) water from the cauliflower and cook until the sauce has thickened, stirring constantly. Mix half the sauce with the vegetable mixture and put it in the bottom of a hot deep flameproof serving dish or casserole. Put the cauliflower on top. Add the grated cheese to the remaining sauce and spoon it over the cauliflower. Brown under the grill (broiler) and serve at once.

Serves 4 to 6

Savoury vegetable strudel

METRIC/IMPERIAL	AMERICAN
175 g./6 oz. flour	1½ cups flour
100 g./4 oz. hard cold butter or margarine	½ cup hard cold butter or margarine
150 ml./¼ pint water	⅝ cup water
5 ml./1 teaspoon vinegar	1 teaspoon vinegar
For the filling	**For the filling**
30 ml./2 tablespoons oil	2 tablespoons oil
2 onions, chopped	2 onions, chopped
100 g./4 oz. mushrooms	1 cup chopped mushrooms
2 tomatoes, skinned and chopped	2 tomatoes, skinned and chopped
350 g./12 oz. frozen spinach	12 oz. frozen spinach
15 ml./1 tablespoon chopped nuts or sesame seeds	1 tablespoon chopped nuts or sesame seeds
2.5 ml./½ teaspoon salt	½ teaspoon salt
pinch of pepper	pinch of pepper
pinch of dried mixed herbs	pinch of dried mixed herbs
pinch of garlic salt	pinch of garlic salt
15 ml./1 tablespoon parsley	1 tablespoon chopped parsley
For topping	**For topping**
22 ml./1½ tablespoons melted butter	1½ tablespoons melted butter
25 g./1 oz. dry breadcrumbs	¼ cup dry breadcrumbs
extra nuts or sesame seeds	extra nuts or sesame seeds

First make the pastry dough. Sift the flour into a bowl and add the butter or margarine cut into large pieces. Mix with water and vinegar, adding enough to make a soft dough. Roll out the dough into an oblong and fold it in three, then seal the edges and turn to the left. Repeat this procedure twice, then refrigerate.

To make the filling, heat the oil in a pan and fry the onions until a pale brown. Add the mushrooms, tomatoes and spinach. Add the rest of the filling ingredients and cook for about 10 minutes or until the spinach is cooked and liquid has evaporated. Leave the mixture to cool.

Cut the dough in two, roll it out thinly into an oblong and brush with one-third of the melted butter and half the breadcrumbs. Spread half the filling to within 2.5 cm./1 in. of the edge of the dough. Wet the edges, roll up, brush with melted butter and sprinkle with nuts or sesame seeds. Repeat with the rest of the dough and filling. Place on a greased baking sheet and cook in the oven preheated to hot (220°C/425°F or Gas Mark 7) for 20 to 30 minutes, or until brown.

Serves 4 to 6

Opposite : Cauliflower surprise
Below : Savoury vegetable strudel

105

Rice and vegetable casserole

METRIC/IMPERIAL
1 onion, chopped
2 garlic cloves, chopped
1 green pepper, chopped
45 ml./3 tablespoons olive oil
3 carrots, diced
225 g./8 oz. young green beans, chopped
225 g./8 oz. cooked or canned and drained red kidney beans
15 ml./1 tablespoon chopped parsley
½ kg./1 lb. rice, partly cooked
900 ml./1½ pints vegetable stock
1.25 ml./¼ teaspoon saffron
1.25 ml./¼ teaspoon turmeric
1.25 ml./¼ teaspoon crushed coriander

AMERICAN
1 onion, chopped
2 garlic cloves, chopped
1 green pepper, chopped
3 tablespoons olive oil
3 carrots, diced
8 oz. young green beans, chopped
8 oz. cooked or canned and drained red kidney beans
1 tablespoon chopped parsley
1 lb. rice, partly cooked
3¾ cups vegetable stock
¼ teaspoon saffron
¼ teaspoon turmeric
¼ teaspoon crushed coriander

Fry the onion, garlic and pepper gently in olive oil until soft. Add all the vegetables, parsley and rice and stir. Heat the vegetable stock and stir in the saffron, turmeric and coriander. Add the liquid slowly to the rice mixture. Bring to the boil, reduce heat, cover and cook gently until all the liquid is absorbed, about 20 minutes. Serve hot. *Serves 4 to 6*

Above left : Rice and vegetable casserole
Above right : Vegetable casserole
Opposite : Cabbage and tomato casserole

Vegetable casserole

METRIC/IMPERIAL	AMERICAN
2 large onions, chopped	2 large onions, chopped
2 garlic cloves, chopped	2 garlic cloves, chopped
vegetable oil for frying	vegetable oil for frying
2 green peppers, chopped	2 green peppers, chopped
$\frac{1}{2}$ kg./1 lb. courgettes, sliced	1 lb. zucchini, sliced and salted
2 medium aubergines, sliced, salted and drained	2 medium eggplants, sliced, salted and drained
225 g./8 oz. mushrooms, sliced	8 oz. mushrooms, sliced
$\frac{1}{2}$ kg./1 lb. ripe tomatoes, skinned and chopped	1 lb. ripe tomatoes, skinned and chopped
1 small can tomato purée	1 small can tomato purée
2 bay leaves	2 bay leaves
15 ml./1 tablespoon chopped parsley	1 tablespoon chopped parsley
2.5 ml./$\frac{1}{2}$ teaspoon dried oregano	$\frac{1}{2}$ teaspoon dried oregano
2.5 ml./$\frac{1}{2}$ teaspoon dried thyme	$\frac{1}{2}$ teaspoon dried thyme
2 large potatoes, thinly sliced	2 large potatoes, thinly sliced
wheatgerm (optional)	wheatgerm (optional)
25 g./1 oz. butter or margarine	2 tablespoons butter or margarine

Fry the onions and garlic in oil in a large heavy pan. Add peppers, courgettes (zucchini), aubergines (eggplants), and mushrooms and cook for a few minutes. Then tip the vegetables into a deep ovenproof casserole and add the tomatoes, tomato purée and the herbs. Top with a layer of potato slices and sprinkle with wheatgerm if liked. Dot with butter or margarine and bake in the oven preheated to moderate (180°C/350°F or Gas Mark 4) for about 1 hour, or until the potatoes are soft underneath and crisp and brown on top. Serve hot. *Serves 4*

Cabbage and tomato casserole

METRIC/IMPERIAL	AMERICAN
50 g./2 oz. butter	$\frac{1}{4}$ cup butter
1 onion, grated	1 onion, grated
1 small apple, grated	1 small apple, grated
4 large tomatoes, skinned and chopped	4 large tomatoes, skinned and chopped
150 ml./$\frac{1}{4}$ pint water	$\frac{5}{8}$ cup water
salt and pepper	salt and pepper
$\frac{1}{2}$ small cabbage, shredded and cooked	$\frac{1}{2}$ small cabbage, shredded and cooked
100 g./4 oz. Cheddar cheese, grated	1 cup grated Cheddar cheese
50 g./2 oz. dry breadcrumbs	$\frac{1}{2}$ cup dry breadcrumbs

Melt the butter in a large pan and gently cook the onion, apple and tomatoes. Add the water and seasoning and simmer to a thick purée. Add the cabbage and heat through. Put in a flameproof dish, sprinkle with the cheese and crumbs and brown under the grill (broiler). *Serves 4*
To vary, use cauliflower or thickly sliced potato instead of cabbage.

Chick pea (garbanzo) casserole

METRIC/IMPERIAL
225 g./8 oz. chick peas,
   soaked overnight and
   drained
1 garlic clove, chopped
1 onion, chopped
½ kg./1 lb. ripe tomatoes,
   skinned and chopped
225 g./8 oz. cabbage,
   shredded
½ green pepper, chopped
15 ml./1 tablespoon oil
2.5 ml./½ teaspoon ground
   ginger
pinch of ground cloves
1 teaspoon sea salt
freshly ground black pepper
100 ml./4 fl. oz. water or
   vegetable stock

AMERICAN
8 oz. garbanzos, soaked
   overnight and drained
1 garlic clove, chopped
1 onion, chopped
1 lb. ripe tomatoes, skinned
   and chopped
8 oz. cabbage, shredded
½ green pepper, chopped
1 tablespoon oil
½ teaspoon ground ginger
pinch of ground cloves
1 teaspoon sea salt
freshly ground black pepper
½ cup water or vegetable
   stock

Simmer the chick peas (garbanzos) in water for 1½ to 3 hours, or until tender. Fry the garlic and vegetables in oil and season with ginger, cloves, salt and pepper. Add the drained chick peas (garbanzos) to the vegetables and pour in the water or stock.

Place the ingredients in a buttered ovenproof casserole and cook in the oven preheated to moderate (180°C/350°F or Gas Mark 4) for 20 to 30 minutes. Serve hot.   *Serves 4 to 6*

Lentil rissoles

METRIC/IMPERIAL
100 g./4 oz. brown or
   yellow lentils, soaked
   overnight and drained
1 large onion, grated
2 medium potatoes, boiled
   and mashed
75 g./3 oz. fresh
   breadcrumbs
100 g./4 oz. chopped
   almonds
25 g./1 oz. sesame seeds
sea salt
30 ml./2 tablespoons
   chopped parsley
1 egg, beaten

AMERICAN
½ cup brown or yellow
   lentils, soaked overnight
   and drained
1 large onion, grated
2 medium potatoes, boiled
   and mashed
1 cup fresh breadcrumbs
1 cup chopped almonds
2 tablespoons sesame seeds
sea salt
2 tablespoons chopped
   parsley
1 egg, beaten

Bring lentils to the boil in a saucepan of cold salted water. Cover and simmer until they are tender, about 1½ hours. Then drain and mash them and mix with the onion, potatoes, breadcrumbs, nuts, sesame seeds, salt, parsley and egg. Add enough cold water to bind the mixture together.

Form into twelve rissoles, place on a greased baking sheet and bake in the oven preheated to moderate (180°C/350°F or Gas Mark 4) for 25 minutes. If preferred, fry them gently in oil for 15 minutes, or until golden on both sides, turning once. Serve hot with a green vegetable or green salad and tomato sauce.   *Serves 6*

Spinach niçoise

METRIC/IMPERIAL	AMERICAN
1 kg./2 lb. fresh spinach, or about 350 g./12 oz. frozen spinach	2 lb. fresh spinach, or about 12 oz. frozen spinach
salt and pepper	salt and pepper
75 g./3 oz. butter	⅜ cup butter
45 ml./3 tablespoons double cream	3 tablespoons heavy cream
4 large tomatoes, skinned and chopped	4 large tomatoes, skinned and chopped
2 onions, chopped	2 onions, chopped
100 g./4 oz. Cheddar or other hard cheese, grated	1 cup grated Cheddar or other hard cheese
4 hardboiled eggs (optional)	4 hardcooked eggs (optional)

Wash the fresh spinach well and cook in the water clinging to the leaves in a covered pan over gentle heat; add a little salt. Cook frozen spinach as instructed on the packet. Strain the spinach and sieve it or chop it finely. Return it to the pan with half the butter and the cream. Heat gently to a creamy consistency. Add pepper to taste.

While the spinach is cooking, heat the tomatoes and onions in the remaining butter until soft. Add the cheese and season. Put the creamed spinach in a shallow flameproof dish, put the hardboiled eggs on top, if using, then cover with the tomato mixture. Heat for a few minutes under the grill (broiler) and serve immediately. *Serves 4*

Opposite left : Chick pea (garbanzo) casserole
Above : Lentil rissoles
Below : Spinach niçoise

Barbecued chicken drumsticks

METRIC/IMPERIAL
25 g./1 oz. butter, melted
little made mustard
few drops Worcestershire
  or chilli sauce
6 chicken drumsticks

AMERICAN
2 tablespoons butter,
  melted
little made mustard
few drops Worcestershire
  or chili sauce
6 chicken drumsticks

Mix the melted butter with the mustard and Worcestershire or chilli sauce and brush the chicken drumsticks with it. Barbecue over hot coals, turning occasionally, until cooked through. Serve with barbecued sausages and barbecue sauce.

Serves 6

*Opposite : Barbecued chicken
drumsticks and sausages
Below : Barbecued beef saté with
barbecue sauce*

Barbecued beef saté

METRIC/IMPERIAL	AMERICAN
1 kg./2 lb. rump steak, cubed	2 lb. rump steak, cubed
30 ml./2 tablespoons soy sauce	2 tablespoons soy sauce
15 ml./1 tablespoon clear honey	1 tablespoon clear honey
2 garlic cloves, crushed	2 garlic cloves, crushed
5 ml./1 teaspoon ground coriander	1 teaspoon ground coriander
5 ml./1 teaspoon caraway seeds	1 teaspoon caraway seeds
1.25 ml./¼ teaspoon chilli powder	¼ teaspoon chili powder
30 ml./2 tablespoons vegetable oil	2 tablespoons vegetable oil

Place the steak in a large bowl. Mix the remaining ingredients and pour over the meat. Marinate the steak for 1 hour, stirring occasionally. Thread the meat on to six skewers. Barbecue over hot coals, turning occasionally, for 10 minutes or until cooked to taste. Baste with the marinade during cooking. Serve with barbecue sauce. *Serves 4*

Barbecue sauce

METRIC/IMPERIAL	AMERICAN
2 onions, finely chopped	2 onions, finely chopped
30 ml./2 tablespoons brown sugar	2 tablespoons brown sugar
30 ml./2 tablespoons lime or lemon juice	2 tablespoons lime or lemon juice
15 ml./1 tablespoon soy sauce	1 tablespoon soy sauce
100 ml./4 fl. oz. water	½ cup water
100 ml./4 fl. oz. tomato sauce	½ cup tomato sauce
freshly ground black pepper	freshly ground black pepper

Place all the ingredients except the pepper in a pan and heat gently, stirring constantly, until the sugar is dissolved. Add pepper to taste.
Makes about 400 ml./¾ pint (2 cups).

Picnic

Mixed cold meats
Green mayonnaise
Green salad or salad
niçoise
Potato salad
Stuffed French loaf
Fruit and cheese
Serves 4 to 6

Green mayonnaise

METRIC/IMPERIAL	AMERICAN
15 ml./1 tablespoon chopped parsley	1 tablespoon chopped parsley
15 ml./1 tablespoon chopped mint	1 tablespoon chopped mint
1.25 ml./¼ teaspoon chopped fresh tarragon	¼ teaspoon chopped fresh tarragon
1.25 ml./¼ teaspoon chopped fresh thyme	¼ teaspoon chopped fresh thyme
150 ml./¼ pint mayonnaise	⅝ cup mayonnaise

Mix the chopped herbs with the mayonnaise. Use half the mayonnaise for the potato salad and put the rest in a screw-topped jar to serve with the cold meat.

Potato salad

Mix about 350 g./12 oz. diced cooked potatoes with a little French dressing, then with half the green mayonnaise. Sprinkle over 30 ml./2 tablespoons chopped chives or spring onions (scallions), or grated onion.

Salad nicoise

METRIC/IMPERIAL	AMERICAN
1 lettuce	1 lettuce
3 tomatoes	3 tomatoes
2 hardboiled eggs, sliced	2 hardcooked eggs, sliced
225 g./8 oz. cooked new potatoes, sliced (optional)	8 oz. cooked new potatoes, sliced (optional)
225 g./8 oz. cooked green beans	8 oz. cooked green beans
1 × 225 g./8 oz. can tuna fish, drained and flaked	1 × 8 oz. can tuna fish, drained and flaked
1 small can anchovy fillets, drained and separated	1 small can anchovy fillets, drained and separated
mayonnaise or French dressing	mayonnaise or French dressing
salt and pepper	salt and pepper
few black olives	few black olives

Make a salad of the lettuce, tomatoes and eggs. Add the potatoes if used and beans. Then add the tuna fish and anchovy fillets and toss in mayonnaise or French dressing. Add extra seasoning if required. Garnish with black olives.

To take the salad on a picnic, pack the lettuce, tomatoes, eggs, potatoes and cooked beans in a plastic box. Leave the tuna fish and anchovy fillets in cans, put the dressing in a screw-topped jar and pack the olives separately. Assemble the salad just before eating. Serve with French bread.

Stuffed French loaf

METRIC/IMPERIAL	AMERICAN
For each French loaf:	For each French loaf:
50 g./2 oz. butter	¼ cup butter
5–10 ml./1–2 teaspoons made mustard	1–2 teaspoons made mustard
30 ml./2 tablespoons tomato ketchup	2 tablespoons tomato ketchup
15 ml./1 tablespoon chopped gherkins	1 tablespoon chopped dill pickle
15–30 ml./1–2 tablespoons chopped spring onions or chives	1–2 tablespoons chopped scallions or chives
350 g./12 oz. liver sausage or cooked minced beef	12 oz. liver sausage or cooked ground beef

Cream the butter and mix it with all the other ingredients. Split the loaf lengthways and spread thinly with butter. Spread on the filling and reshape the loaf. Wrap the loaf in foil to take it to the picnic, or pack the filling, butter and loaf separately and put together just before eating.

Haddock charlotte with creamed carrots and Duchesse potatoes
Peach madrilènes
Serves 4

Haddock charlotte

METRIC/IMPERIAL	AMERICAN
550 g./1¼ lb. fresh haddock, cooked and flaked	1¼ lb. fresh haddock, cooked and flaked
1 egg, beaten	1 egg, beaten
150 ml./¼ pint milk	⅝ cup milk
salt and pepper	salt and pepper
5 ml./1 teaspoon finely grated lemon rind	1 teaspoon finely grated lemon rind
5 ml./1 teaspoon finely chopped parsley	1 teaspoon finely chopped parsley
4–5 large slices bread, crusts removed and buttered	4–5 large slices bread, crusts removed and buttered
For the garnish	**For the garnish**
tomato slices	tomato slices
lemon wedges	lemon wedges

Mix the flaked fish with the egg, milk, seasoning, lemon rind and parsley. Cut the bread into fingers and cover the bottom of a 1.1 l./2 pint pie dish with a layer of bread, buttered side down. Spoon the fish mixture over the bread and top with a layer of bread fingers, buttered side up. Bake in the centre of the oven preheated to moderate (180°C/350°F or Gas Mark 4) until the topping is crisp. Garnish with tomato slices and lemon wedges.

Creamed carrots

METRIC/IMPERIAL	AMERICAN
½ kg./1 lb. carrots	1 lb. carrots
knob of butter	knob of butter
30 ml./2 tablespoons single cream	2 tablespoons light cream
chopped parsley to garnish	chopped parsley to garnish

Cook the carrots until tender, then mash them well. Mix mashed carrots with the butter and cream and pile into a serving dish. Garnish with chopped parsley.

Duchesse potatoes

METRIC/IMPERIAL	AMERICAN
700 g.(1½ lb. potatoes	1½ lb. potatoes
50 g./2 oz. butter	¼ cup butter
1 or 2 egg yolks	1 or 2 egg yolks

Cook and mash the potatoes, then sieve them to remove any lumps. Beat the butter and the egg yolks into the mashed potato. Do not add milk as it makes the potato shapes spread out. Pipe the potatoes into rose shapes, or pile in pyramid shapes, on to a greased baking pan. Heat through and brown in the moderate oven with the haddock.

Peach madrilènes

METRIC/IMPERIAL	AMERICAN
1 orange, divided into segments	1 orange, divided into segments
150 ml./¼ pint double cream	⅝ cup heavy cream
caster sugar	superfine sugar
12 grapes, halved and seeded	12 grapes, halved and seeded
2 large peaches or 4 small ones, halved and stoned	2 large peaches or 4 small ones, halved and pitted

**Harlequin soufflé omelet
with broccoli
Hot melon with ginger**
Serves 4

Harlequin soufflé omelet

METRIC/IMPERIAL	AMERICAN
8 eggs, separated	8 eggs, separated
225 g./8 oz. cottage cheese, sieved	8 oz. cottage cheese, sieved
salt and pepper	salt and pepper
15 ml./1 tablespoon chopped parsley	1 tablespoon chopped parsley
30 ml./2 tablespoons chopped chives or spring onions	2 tablespoons chopped chives or scallions
50 g./2 oz. butter	¼ cup butter
For the garnish	**For the garnish**
1 red pepper, sliced	1 red pepper, sliced
1 green pepper, sliced	1 green pepper, sliced

Beat the egg yolks with the cottage cheese and seasoning until smooth. Add the parsley and chives or spring onions (scallions). Then fold in the stiffly beaten egg whites.

Melt the butter in a very ~~~~ two omelets in a smaller pan) ~~~~ mixture and cook steadily for about 5 minut~~~~ underside is golden. Then cook under a medium g~~~~) for 3 to 4 minutes, until set. Slide the omelet out of pan on to a hot dish (do not fold the omelet). Garnish with pepper rings and serve at once.

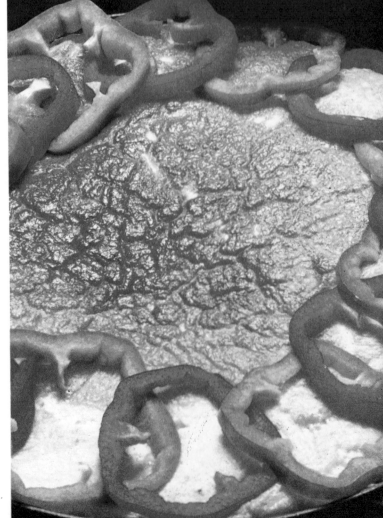

Remove the skin, pith and pips (seeds) from the orange segments and cut the fruit into neat pieces. Whip the cream until it just holds its shape and sweeten to taste. Add the grapes and orange segments and pile the mixture into the peach halves.

To vary, thick smooth custard, soured cream or natural yogurt may be used in place of cream.

Harlequin soufflé omelet

Broccoli

METRIC/IMPERIAL
700 g./1½ lb. broccoli
salt
melted butter

AMERICAN
1½ lb. broccoli
salt
melted butter

Cook the broccoli in boiling salted water, or steam it, until tender (10 to 12 minutes). Toss the broccoli in melted butter and place it in a serving dish.

Hot melon with ginger

METRIC/IMPERIAL
1 ripe melon, sliced and
  seeded
juice of ½ orange
little ground ginger

AMERICAN
1 ripe melon, sliced and
  seeded
juice of ½ orange
little ground ginger

Moisten the melon slices with the orange juice and sprinkle with a little ground ginger. Warm the melon in the oven preheated to moderate (180°C/350°F or Gas Mark 4) for about 20 minutes. Serve hot.

Broccoli and Hot melon with ginger

**Tomato juice cocktail
Savoury cheese log with
garlic bread and salad
Pineapple soufflé
pudding**
Serves 4 to 6

Tomato juice cocktail

METRIC/IMPERIAL
600 ml./1 pint tomato juice
shake of celery salt
pinch of cayenne pepper
little Worcestershire sauce
few bruised mint leaves
To decorate glasses
1 egg white, lightly beaten
very finely chopped mint or
  parsley

AMERICAN
2½ cups tomato juice
shake of celery salt
pinch of cayenne pepper
little Worcestershire sauce
few bruised mint leaves
To decorate glasses
1 egg white, lightly beaten
very finely chopped mint or
  parsley

Mix the tomato juice with the seasoning, Worcestershire sauce and mint leaves. Chill.

To decorate the glasses, dip the rims in beaten egg white, then in the chopped mint or parsley.

Savoury cheese log

METRIC/IMPERIAL
½ kg./1 lb. Cheddar or other
  hard cheese, finely grated
30 ml./2 tablespoons each of
  diced cucumber, sliced
  stuffed olives, sliced
  radishes and chopped
  walnuts
mayonnaise
For the garnish
sliced olives
halved walnuts
sliced radishes
salad

AMERICAN
1 lb. Cheddar or other hard
  cheese, finely grated
2 tablespoons each of diced
  cucumber, sliced stuffed
  olives, sliced radishes and
  chopped walnuts
mayonnaise
For the garnish
sliced olives
halved walnuts
sliced radishes
salad

Mix the grated cheese with the cucumber, olives, radishes and walnuts. Moisten with enough mayonnaise to make the consistency of very thick whipped cream. Form into a long roll. Garnish with olives, walnuts and radishes and chill well. Arrange the salad round the cheese log on a serving dish.

Garlic bread

Slice a French loaf almost to the base, without cutting right through. Blend 50 g./2 oz. (¼ cup) butter with garlic salt or crushed garlic and spread it on the bread slices. Wrap the loaf in foil and heat in the oven preheated to moderate (180°C/350°F or Gas Mark 4) for 25 to 30 minutes.

Pineapple soufflé pudding

METRIC/IMPERIAL	AMERICAN
50 g./2 oz. butter	¼ cup butter
50 g./2 oz. caster sugar	¼ cup superfine sugar
grated rind and juice of 1 lemon	grated rind and juice of 1 lemon
2 eggs, separated	2 eggs, separated
50 g./2 oz. self-raising flour, sifted	½ cup self-rising flour, sifted
175 ml./6 fl. oz. canned pineapple juice	¾ cup canned pineapple juice

Cream the butter with the sugar and lemon rind. Gradually beat in the egg yolks and flour. Add the lemon and pineapple juices. Fold in the stiffly beaten egg whites. The mixture may look curdled at this stage, but it does not matter.

Pour the mixture into a soufflé dish or pie dish and stand it in a roasting pan containing a little cold water. Bake in the centre of the oven preheated to moderate (180°C/350°F or Gas Mark 4) for about 40 minutes, or until risen and light brown. Serve hot.

The pudding separates during cooking, giving a sauce layer at the bottom of the dish with a light soufflé mixture on the top.

To vary, serve with rings of hot pineapple or with vanilla ice cream. Use orange juice in place of pineapple juice.

Speedy bortsch
Sweet and sour ham with
crisp-topped noodles
Green beans and
tomatoes
Cherry grapefruit Alaska
Serves 4

Speedy bortsch

METRIC/IMPERIAL	AMERICAN
1 medium onion, chopped	1 medium onion, chopped
small knob of fat	small knob of fat
900 ml./1½ pints canned consommé	3¾ cups canned consommé
salt and pepper	salt and pepper
1 large cooked beetroot, grated	1 large cooked beet, grated
yogurt or soured cream for garnish	yogurt or sour cream for garnish

Fry the onion in the melted fat until it is soft but not brown. Add the consommé and heat thoroughly. Season well. Add the beetroot (beet) and heat it through. Spoon the soup into individual bowls and top with a little yogurt or soured cream.

Sweet and sour ham

METRIC/IMPERIAL	AMERICAN
40 g./1½ oz. butter	3 tablespoons butter
25 g./1 oz. brown sugar	2½ tablespoons brown sugar
45 ml./3 tablespoons vinegar	3 tablespoons vinegar
45 ml./3 tablespoons redcurrant jelly	3 tablespoons redcurrant jelly
5–10 ml./1–2 teaspoons made mustard	1–2 teaspoons made mustard
good shake of pepper	good shake of pepper
4 slices cooked ham, 6–12 mm./¼–½ in. thick	4 slices cooked ham, ¼–½ in. thick

Put the butter, brown sugar, vinegar and redcurrant jelly in a frying pan and stir over gentle heat until the mixture forms a smooth sauce. Add the mustard and pepper. Add a little salt if the ham is mild in flavour. Put in the slices of ham and heat gently. Serve the ham on crisp-topped noodles and spoon over the sauce.

To vary, add a few drops of Worcestershire sauce or Tabasco sauce.

Crisp-topped noodles

METRIC/IMPERIAL	AMERICAN
225 g./8 oz. noodles	8 oz. noodles
small knob of butter	small knob of butter
50 g./2 oz. dry breadcrumbs	½ cup dry breadcrumbs
50 g./2 oz. grated cheese	½ cup grated cheese

Cook the noodles in boiling salted water until tender, then drain them. Toss the noodles in the butter in a heatproof dish and top with the breadcrumbs and cheese. Brown for a few minutes under the grill (broiler) or in the oven.

Green beans and tomatoes

METRIC/IMPERIAL	AMERICAN
½ kg./1 lb. frozen or fresh green beans	1 lb. frozen or fresh green beans
3–4 tomatoes, skinned and sliced	3–4 tomatoes, skinned and sliced
salt and pepper	salt and pepper

Cook the beans in boiling salted water until tender. Drain the beans and put them in a pan with the tomatoes and seasoning. Heat for a few minutes and serve.

To vary, fry a chopped onion in butter for 5 minutes, then add the cooked beans and the tomatoes to the pan and turn them in the onion and butter. Alternatively, add chopped fresh herbs to the pan with the tomatoes.

Cherry grapefruit Alaska

METRIC/IMPERIAL	AMERICAN
2 good-sized grapefruit	2 good-sized grapefruit
1 small can black cherries, drained	1 small can black cherries, drained
3 egg whites	3 egg whites
100 g./4 oz. caster sugar	½ cup superfine sugar
vanilla ice cream	vanilla ice cream

Cut the grapefruit in half and remove the segments. Discard the pith, the skin around the segments and the pips (seeds). Put the grapefruit pieces back in the cases with some of the cherries and sweeten to taste. Whisk the egg whites until very stiff and gradually whisk in the sugar. Place a scoop of ice cream on each grapefruit half and spoon over the meringue mixture. Decorate with a few cherries. Bake in the oven pre-heated to very hot (230°C/450°F or Gas Mark 8) for 5 minutes.

To vary, use halved and seeded grapes in place of cherries.

**Citrus fruit cocktails
Grilled sole and
cauliflower niçoise
Gingerbread with
apple sauce**
Serves 4

Citrus fruit cocktails

METRIC/IMPERIAL	AMERICAN
juice of 1 large grapefruit	juice of 1 large grapefruit
juice of ½ lemon	juice of ½ lemon
juice of 4 large oranges	juice of 4 large oranges
sugar or honey to taste	sugar or honey to taste
few bruised mint leaves if available	few bruised mint leaves, if available

Mix all the fruit juices and sweeten to taste with sugar or honey. Add a few bruised mint leaves if available. Serve in stemmed glasses.

Note: If you wish to frost the glasses, dip the rims in lightly beaten egg white, then in white sugar.

Cauliflower niçoise

METRIC/IMPERIAL	AMERICAN
1 medium cauliflower, in florets	1 medium cauliflower, in florets
salt and pepper	salt and pepper
50 g./2 oz. butter	¼ cup butter
2 onions, chopped	2 onions, chopped
4 large tomatoes, skinned and chopped	4 large tomatoes, skinned and chopped
5 ml./1 teaspoon cornflour	1 teaspoon cornstarch
2 anchovy fillets, chopped	2 anchovy fillets, chopped

Cook the cauliflower in boiling salted water until tender. Meanwhile melt the butter in a pan and cook the onions until soft. Add the tomatoes and cook to a thick purée. Mix the cornflour (cornstarch) with about 150 ml./¼ pint (⅝ cup) of the cauliflower water and add it to the tomato mixture with the anchovy fillets. Cook until thickened and spoon the sauce over the cauliflower.

Note: Green beans may also be served in this way.

Grilled sole

METRIC/IMPERIAL	AMERICAN
4 medium sole, soaked in a little milk for 30 minutes	4 medium sole, soaked in a little milk for 30 minutes
butter	butter
For the garnish	**For the garnish**
parsley sprigs	parsley sprigs
lemon wedges	lemon wedges

Drain the fish and brush with melted butter. Grill (broil) on both sides until tender. Garnish with parsley sprigs and lemon wedges.

Gingerbread

METRIC/IMPERIAL	AMERICAN
225 g./8 oz. flour	2 cups flour
3.75 ml./¾ teaspoon bicarbonate of soda	¾ teaspoon baking soda
5 ml./1 teaspoon ground cinnamon	1 teaspoon ground cinnamon
10 ml./2 teaspoons ground ginger	2 teaspoons ground ginger
100 g./4 oz. butter	½ cup butter
100 g./4 oz. dark brown sugar	⅔ cup dark brown sugar
150 g./5 oz. black treacle	⅔ cup plus 2 tablespoons molasses
2 eggs, beaten	2 eggs, beaten
60 ml./4 tablespoons milk	4 tablespoons milk

Sift the dry ingredients together into a large mixing bowl. Melt the butter in a pan with the sugar and treacle (molasses), then add the mixture to the flour. Beat in the eggs and milk. Pour the mixture into a 10 cm./8 in. square tin lined with greased greaseproof (waxed) paper. Bake in the centre of the oven preheated to warm (170°C/325°F or Gas Mark 3) for 1¼ hours. Let the cake cool in the tin. Cut into squares for serving. Serve apple sauce separately.

Apple sauce

Simmer ½ kg./1 lb. sliced apples in a little water with sugar to taste. Sieve or purée in a blender.

Desserts

Berry mould

METRIC/IMPERIAL	AMERICAN
225 g./8 oz. strawberries, hulled	8 oz. strawberries, hulled
½ kg./1 lb. black cherries, stoned	1 lb. black cherries, pitted
2 cooking apples, peeled, cored and sliced	2 cooking apples, peeled, cored and sliced
175–225 g./6–8 oz. caster sugar	¾–1 cup superfine sugar
6–8 slices white bread, crusts removed	6–8 slices white bread, crusts removed
cream for serving	cream for serving

Keep a few strawberries and cherries for decoration. Put the rest of the fruit in a pan with the sugar. Cover and heat very gently until the juices run from the fruit. Stir occasionally to prevent the fruit from sticking.

Line a 1 l./2 pint pudding bowl with the slices of bread, keeping some bread for the top. Fill the lined bowl with the fruit and cover with bread. Place a saucer or small plate on top of the pudding, press it down until the juice comes to the surface, then put a weight on it. Chill overnight. Turn out, decorate with reserved fruit and serve with cream.

Serves 4 to 6

Mocha pots

METRIC/IMPERIAL	AMERICAN
6 eggs, separated	6 eggs, separated
25 g./1 oz. butter	2 tablespoons butter
175 g./6 oz. plain chocolate	6 oz. (6 squares) semi-sweet chocolate
22 ml./1½ tablespoons rum	1½ tablespoons rum
45 ml./3 tablespoons coffee essence	3 tablespoons coffee essence
45 ml./3 tablespoons double cream	3 tablespoons heavy cream

Put the egg yolks, butter and chocolate in a heatproof bowl placed over a pan of hot water. Cook gently, stirring occasionally, until the chocolate has melted. Remove the bowl from the heat and beat in the rum and coffee essence.

Whisk the egg whites until stiff and fold them into the chocolate mixture. Pour into eight small ramekin dishes or pots and leave in a cool place to set. Whisk the cream until thick and decorate each pot. Serve with crisp sweet biscuits (cookies).

Serves 8

Stuffed figs

METRIC/IMPERIAL	AMERICAN
4 ripe fresh figs	4 ripe fresh figs
225 g./8 oz. Ricotto, cottage or cream cheese	1 cup Ricotto, cottage or cream cheese
1 large egg, separated	1 large egg, separated
50 g./2 oz. sugar	¼ cup sugar
15–30 ml./1–2 tablespoons kirsch or brandy	1–2 tablespoons kirsch or brandy
almonds to decorate	almonds to decorate

Wipe the figs and cut downwards into quarters, just enough to be able to open out the fruit–take care not to cut right through. Put the cheese in a mixing bowl; if using cottage cheese, sieve it. Add the egg yolk and sugar to the cheese and beat until the mixture is light and creamy. Then add the kirsch or brandy.

Beat the egg white until it is stiff and fold it into the cheese. Spoon the mixture into the centre of the figs and decorate each one with an almond. Chill before serving. *Serves 4*

Orange cheesecake

METRIC/IMPERIAL	AMERICAN
50 g./2 oz. butter	¼ cup butter
15 ml./1 tablespoon clear honey	1 tablespoon clear honey
grated rind of 2 oranges	grated rind of 2 oranges
50 g./2 oz. caster sugar	¼ cup superfine sugar
175 g./6 oz. digestive biscuits, crushed	6 oz. graham crackers, crushed
For the filling	**For the filling**
50 g./2 oz. butter	¼ cup butter
grated rind of 1 orange	grated rind of 1 orange
75 g./3 oz. caster sugar	⅜ cup superfine sugar
2 eggs, separated	2 eggs, separated
25 g./1 oz. cornflour	¼ cup cornstarch
350 g./12 oz. cottage cheese, sieved	12 oz. cottage cheese, sieved
30 ml./2 tablespoons orange juice	2 tablespoons orange juice
For decoration	**For decoration**
little sifted icing sugar	little sifted confectioners' sugar
can of mandarin oranges, drained	can of mandarin oranges, drained

To make the flan case, cream the butter, honey, orange rind and sugar together. Mix in the crumbs and press into a 10 cm./8 in. cake tin with a removable base. To make the filling, cream the butter, orange rind and sugar together. Mix in the egg yolks, cornflour (cornstarch), cottage cheese and orange juice. Then fold in the stiffly whisked egg whites. Spoon the mixture into the crumb case and bake in the centre of the oven preheated to warm (170°C/325°F or Gas Mark 3) for about 1¼ hours, or until firm and pale golden. Leave the cake to cool in the oven with the heat turned off (to prevent it sinking). Remove the cake from the tin. Sprinkle with icing (confectioners') sugar and decorate with drained mandarin oranges. *Serves 6 to 8*

Apple charlotte

METRIC/IMPERIAL	AMERICAN
½ kg./1 lb. cooking apples	1 lb. cooking apples
juice of ½ lemon	juice of ½ lemon
50 g./2 oz. butter or margarine	¼ cup butter or margarine
75 g./3 oz. fresh breadcrumbs	1 cup fresh breadcrumbs
75 g./3 oz. brown sugar	⅜ cup brown sugar
2.5 ml./½ teaspoon cinnamon	½ teaspoon cinnamon
grated rind of ½ lemon	grated rind of ½ lemon
15 ml./1 tablespoon water	1 tablespoon water
For decoration	**For decoration**
1 red dessert apple	1 red dessert apple
extra lemon juice and rind	extra lemon juice and rind

Peel the cooking apples, grate them coarsely and sprinkle with lemon juice. Grease a pie dish with some of the margarine or butter. Mix the breadcrumbs, sugar, cinnamon and lemon rind and put a third of it in the base of the pie dish. Cover with half the apples, then sprinkle with a third of the crumb mixture and dot with half the remaining butter or margarine. Cover with the rest of the apples and add the water. Sprinkle with the rest of the crumb mixture and dot with the remaining butter or margarine. Cover with foil and bake in the oven preheated to fairly hot (200°C/400°F or Gas Mark 6) for about 45 minutes, then remove the foil to brown. Decorate with apple slices dipped in lemon juice and strips of lemon rind. *Serves 3*

Above : Stuffed figs
Opposite top : Apple charlotte
Opposite bottom : Orange cheesecake

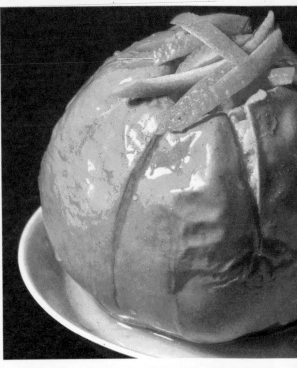

Caramel custard

METRIC/IMPERIAL	AMERICAN
75 g./3 oz. caster sugar	¾ cup superfine sugar
45 ml./3 tablespoons water	3 tablespoons water
For the custard	**For the custard**
600 ml./1 pint milk	2½ cups milk
4 eggs	4 eggs
15 ml./1 tablespoon sugar	1 tablespoon sugar

To make the caramel sauce, put the caster (superfine) sugar in a heavy pan with the water. Stir over very low heat until the sugar dissolves. If the sugar and water splash against the sides of the pan, brush with a pastry brush dipped in cold water – this helps prevent the mixture crystallizing. Allow the sugar and water to boil steadily until golden brown, then use it to coat a 10 cm./8 in. oval or round ovenproof dish. Turn the dish round to make sure the bottom and sides are evenly coated.

To make the custard, heat the milk in a pan to blood temperature – do not let it boil. Beat the eggs and sugar together in a bowl, then add the heated milk, stirring constantly. Pour the custard into the caramel-coated dish and stand it in a baking pan containing cold water. Bake in the coolest part of the oven preheated to cool (150°C/300°F or Gas Mark 2) for 1½ to 2 hours until the custard is firm. Leave it to cool in the dish for about 10 minutes, then invert it on to a serving dish.

Serves 4 to 6

Baked apples with orange filling

METRIC/IMPERIAL	AMERICAN
4 large cooking apples	4 large cooking apples
30 ml./2 tablespoons orange marmalade	2 tablespoons orange marmalade
finely grated rind of 1 orange	finely grated rind of 1 orange
30 ml./2 tablespoons orange juice	2 tablespoons orange juice
sugar to taste	sugar to taste
strips of orange rind to decorate	strips of orange rind to decorate

Remove the cores from the apples and make a slight slit in the skin round the centre to stop the apples bursting. Place the apples in an ovenproof dish and fill the centres with the marmalade, orange rind and juice. Add sugar to taste.

Bake the apples in the centre of the oven preheated to moderate (180°C/350°F or Gas Mark 4) for about 1 hour. Decorate with strips of orange rind.

Serves 4

Above left : Caramel custard
Above right : Baked apples with orange filling
Opposite left : Banana and lemon cream
Opposite right : Orange water ice

Banana and lemon cream

METRIC/IMPERIAL	AMERICAN
1 packet lemon-flavoured jelly	1 packet lemon-flavoured powdered gelatin
400 ml./¾ pint boiling water	1⅞ cups boiling water
20 ml./4 teaspoons lemon juice	4 teaspoons lemon juice
15 ml./1 tablespoon caster sugar	1 tablespoon superfine sugar
300 ml./½ pint double cream	1¼ cups heavy cream
2 egg whites, stiffly beaten	2 egg whites, stiffly beaten
5 small bananas	5 small bananas
20–24 sponge finger biscuits	20–24 sponge finger cookies
few glacé cherries	few candied cherries

Dissolve the jelly (gelatin) in the water and stir in half the lemon juice and all the sugar. Cool until it is just beginning to set. To set it more quickly, stand the bowl over ice cubes, or use 150 ml./¼ pint (⅞ cup) hot water to dissolve the jelly (gelatin) and make up the quantity with iced water. When the jelly is firm, whip it until frothy, then add most of the cream, whipped until stiff. Fold in the egg whites and three sliced bananas. Spoon into a 1 l./2 pint (5 cup) tin or mould (rinsed in cold water). When set, turn out. Press cream-coated sponge fingers round the edge and top with the remaining whipped cream, sliced bananas (dipped in the remaining lemon juice) and the glacé cherries. *Serves 6*

Orange water ice

METRIC/IMPERIAL	AMERICAN
thinly pared rind and juice of 3 large oranges	thinly pared rind and juice of 3 large oranges
thinly pared rind and juice of 1 small lemon	thinly pared rind and juice of 1 small lemon
400 ml./¾ pint water	2 cups water
100 g./4 oz. sugar	½ cup sugar
10 ml./2 teaspoons powdered gelatine	2 teaspoons powdered gelatin
1 egg white	1 egg white

Put the orange and lemon rind in a pan with the water and sugar and simmer for 8 minutes. Soften the gelatine in 30 ml./2 tablespoons orange juice and add it to the pan, stirring until it is dissolved. Then strain the liquid and add it to the remaining fruit juice. Taste and add a little extra sugar if required, but do not make the mixture too sweet.

When the mixture is cool, pour it into a freezing tray and freeze it in the frozen food compartment of a refrigerator or in a freezer. When it is lightly frosted, remove it and blend it with the stiffly beaten egg white. Freeze again until firm. Serve in glasses or in orange skins as illustrated. *Serves 6*

Above : Fruit meringue trifle; Below : Apricot fool

Fruit meringue trifle

METRIC/IMPERIAL
700 g./1½ lb. raspberries
sugar to taste
400 ml./¾ pint double cream
150 ml./¼ pint white wine
8 medium meringue shells

AMERICAN
1½ lb. raspberries
sugar to taste
2 cups heavy cream
⅝ cup white wine
8 medium meringue shells

Put the raspberries in a bowl and sprinkle with sugar. Whip the cream until it holds its shape. Put a little cream on one side for decoration. Gradually blend the wine with the remain-ing cream and sweeten to taste. Break the meringue shells into fairly large pieces and put a layer at the bottom of a serving bowl. Add half the fruit, then the cream and wine mixture, then most of the remaining fruit–keep a little for decoration. Top with meringue pieces, piped cream and reserved raspberries. Serve within an hour of preparation so that the meringue stays crisp. *Serves 6 to 8*

Note: The trifle can also be made with sliced fresh peaches, apricots or pears–sprinkle them with lemon juice to prevent discoloration.

Apricot fool

METRIC/IMPERIAL
225 g./8 oz. dried apricots,
  soaked overnight in
  300 ml./½ pint water and
  the juice of 1 lemon
sugar to taste
150 ml./¼ pint double cream
  or natural yogurt
flaked browned almonds to
  decorate

AMERICAN
8 oz. dried apricots, soaked
  overnight in 1¼ cups
  water and the juice of
  1 lemon
sugar to taste
⅝ cup heavy cream or
  natural yogurt
flaked browned almonds to
  decorate

Simmer the apricots in the soaking water and lemon juice until they are tender. Sieve them or purée in a blender and sweeten with sugar to taste. Blend the apricot purée with the whipped cream or yogurt. Spoon into four glasses and top with almonds. *Serves 4*

Brigade pudding

Brigade pudding

METRIC/IMPERIAL
225 g./8 oz. self-raising
   flour
pinch of salt
100 g./4 oz. shredded suet
   or butter or margarine
water to mix
For the filling
30 ml./2 tablespoons golden
   syrup
225 g./8 oz. mincemeat
3 large cooking apples,
   cored and grated

AMERICAN
2 cups self-rising flour
pinch of salt
½ cup shredded suet or
   butter or margarine
water to mix
For the filling
2 tablespoons light corn
   syrup
8 oz. mincemeat
3 large cooking apples,
   cored and grated

Sift the flour and salt together. Mix in the suet, or rub in the butter or margarine and bind with enough water to give a rolling consistency. Roll out the dough very thinly. Cut it into four rounds: make one round the size of the base of a pudding bowl of 1 l./2 pints (5 cups) capacity. Make another round almost the size of the top of the bowl and two rounds of intermediate sizes.

Grease the bowl and put the syrup in the bottom, then put in the smallest round of dough. Add one-third of the mincemeat mixed with one-third of the apple. Then put in the next size of dough round topped with mincemeat and apple. Add the third round of dough topped with mincemeat and apple. Top with the largest round of dough and cover with greased paper, then foil. Steam over boiling water for 2½ hours. Turn out and serve with cream. *Serves 6*

129

Pineapple mousse

METRIC/IMPERIAL	AMERICAN
3 eggs, separated	3 eggs, separated
juice of 1 lemon	juice of 1 lemon
50 g./2 oz. caster sugar	$\frac{1}{4}$ cup superfine sugar
12$\frac{1}{2}$ g./$\frac{1}{2}$ oz. powdered gelatine	$\frac{1}{2}$ oz. powdered gelatin
300 ml./$\frac{1}{2}$ pint canned pineapple juice	1$\frac{1}{4}$ cups canned pineapple juice
150 ml./$\frac{1}{4}$ pint double cream	$\frac{5}{8}$ cup heavy cream
extra cream to decorate	extra cream to decorate

Put the egg yolks, lemon juice and sugar in a heatproof bowl over a pan of simmering water and whisk until thick and pale. Remove from the heat and leave to cool, whisking occasionally.

Put the gelatine and 60 ml./4 tablespoons of the pineapple juice in a small heatproof bowl and place over simmering water. Stir to dissolve the gelatine, then add the remaining pineapple juice. Stir into the egg yolk mixture. Leave in a cool place until it is just beginning to set, stirring frequently.

Whisk the cream until it is thick and fold it into the pineapple mixture. Whisk the egg whites until stiff and fold them into the mixture. Turn the mousse into a serving dish and put in the refrigerator to set. Decorate with rosettes of whipped cream.   *Serves 6*

Iced Christmas pudding

METRIC/IMPERIAL	AMERICAN
600 ml./1 pint milk	2$\frac{1}{2}$ cups milk
100 g./4 oz. marshmallows	4 oz. marshmallows
5 ml./1 teaspoon cocoa powder	1 teaspoon cocoa powder
5 ml./1 teaspoon instant coffee powder	1 teaspoon instant coffee powder
50 g./2 oz. raisins	$\frac{1}{2}$ cup raisins
25 g./1 oz. sultanas	$\frac{1}{6}$ cup currants
25 g./1 oz. currants	2 tablespoons sherry
30 ml./2 tablespoons sherry	$\frac{3}{8}$ cup chopped Maraschino cherries
50 g./2 oz. Maraschino cherries, chopped	$\frac{1}{2}$ cup chopped nuts
50 g./2 oz. chopped nuts	1$\frac{1}{4}$ cups heavy cream
300 ml./$\frac{1}{2}$ pint double cream	$\frac{1}{6}$ cup confectioners' sugar, sifted (optional)
25 g./1 oz. icing sugar, sifted (optional)	extra Maraschino cherries to decorate
extra Maraschino cherries to decorate	

Put the milk, marshmallows, cocoa and coffee into a pan and heat gently until the marshmallows are almost melted. Then allow to cool. Meanwhile mix the dried fruit with the sherry. Leave the fruit to stand for 30 minutes, then add it to the marshmallow mixture with the cherries and nuts. Freeze for a short time until the mixture is slightly thickened. Then fold in the whipped cream and turn the mixture into a chilled bowl. Freeze until firm.

Turn the pudding out, sprinkle with icing (confectioners') sugar if used, decorate with cherries and serve with whipped cream and crisp biscuits (cookies).   *Serves 6*

Opposite bottom : Iced Christmas pudding ; Above left ; Pineapple mousse ; Above right : Chilled raspberry cheesecake

Chilled raspberry cheesecake

METRIC/IMPERIAL	AMERICAN
1 packet lemon-flavoured jelly	1 packet lemon-flavoured powdered gelatin
175 g./6 oz. digestive biscuits, crushed	6 oz. graham crackers, crushed
25 g./1 oz. Demerara sugar	2 tablespoons light brown sugar
75 g./3 oz. butter, melted	3/8 cup butter, melted
150 ml./1/4 pint double cream	5/8 cup heavy cream
350 g./12 oz. rich cream cheese	12 oz. rich cream cheese
juice of 2 lemons	juice of 2 lemons
100 g./4 oz. caster sugar	1/2 cup superfine sugar
For the topping	**For the topping**
225 g./8 oz. raspberries, frozen or fresh	8 oz. raspberries, frozen or fresh
60 ml./4 tablespoons redcurrant jelly	4 tablespoons redcurrant jelly

Dissolve the jelly (gelatine) in 150 ml./1/4 pint (5/8 cup) boiling water. Make up to 300 ml./1/2 pint (1 1/4 cups) with cold water and leave to become cold, thick and nearly set. Mix the crushed biscuits (crackers), Demerara (brown) sugar and melted butter and use the mixture to line the bottom of a 20 to 22.5 cm./8 to 9 in. diameter spring mould.

Whisk the cream until thick. Mash the cream cheese, then gradually beat in the thickened jelly (gelatine), lemon juice, cream and caster (superfine) sugar. Turn the mixture into the prepared mould and put in the refrigerator to set.

About 30 minutes before serving, arrange the raspberries around the edge of the cheesecake. Melt the redcurrant jelly over low heat and spoon it over the cheesecake. If necessary, thin the jelly with a little water. *Serves 6*

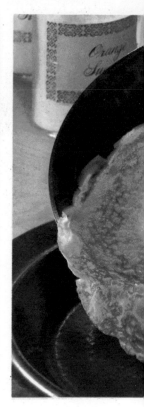

Above : Christmas pudding ; Centre : Pancakes (crêpes) ; Right : Lemon soufflé

Christmas pudding

METRIC/IMPERIAL

100 g./4 oz. self-raising
  flour
5 ml./1 teaspoon ground
  mixed spice
2.5 ml./½ teaspoon
  powdered cinnamon
2.5 ml./½ teaspoon grated
  nutmeg
100 g./4 oz. soft fine
  breadcrumbs
100 g./4 oz. shredded suet
100 g./4 oz. dark brown
  sugar
350 g./12 oz. seedless
  raisins
100 g./4 oz. sultanas
100 g./4 oz. currants
100 g./4 oz. chopped
  candied peel
50 g./2 oz. chopped
  blanched almonds
100 g./4 oz. grated cooking
  apple
grated rind and juice of
  1 lemon
2 eggs, beaten
150 ml./¼ pint beer to mix
30 ml./2 tablespoons
  brandy or sherry

AMERICAN

1 cup self-rising flour
1 teaspoon ground mixed
  spice
½ teaspoon powdered
  cinnamon
½ teaspoon grated nutmeg
1½ cups soft fine
  breadcrumbs
4 oz. shredded suet
⅔ cup dark brown sugar
2⅔ cups seedless raisins
⅔ cup currants
⅔ cup chopped candied peel
½ cup chopped blanched
  almonds
⅔ cup grated cooking apple
grated rind and juice of
  1 lemon
2 eggs, beaten
⅞ cup ale to mix
2 tablespoons brandy or
  sherry

Sift the flour with the spices into a large mixing bowl. Add the breadcrumbs, suet and sugar. Mix in the fruit, nuts, apple, lemon rind and juice. Then add the eggs with the beer and mix well. Finally, mix in the brandy or sherry.

Divide the mixture between two or three greased pudding bowls. Cover the top of each bowl with greased foil or grease-proof (waxed) paper, making a pleat in the top to allow for expansion. Steam over boiling water for at least 5 hours. Then remove the wet covers and put on dry foil or greaseproof (waxed) paper covers and store in a cool, dry place.

Cook the puddings in the same way for 2 to 3 hours before serving. Serve with brandy butter.   *Makes 2 to 3 puddings*

Brandy butter

METRIC/IMPERIAL

100 g./4 oz. unsalted
  butter
225 g./8 oz. icing sugar,
  sifted
60 ml./4 tablespoons
  brandy

AMERICAN

½ cup unsalted butter
1⅓ cups confectioners'
  sugar, sifted
4 tablespoons brandy

Cream the butter and sugar together, then mix in the brandy. Chill thoroughly before serving.   *Serves 8 to 10*

Pancakes (crêpes)

METRIC/IMPERIAL	AMERICAN
100 g./4 oz. flour	1 cup flour
pinch of salt	pinch of salt
2 eggs, beaten	2 eggs, beaten
300 ml./½ pint milk, or milk and water	1¼ cups milk, or milk and water
10 ml./2 teaspoons melted butter or oil	2 teaspoons melted butter or oil
oil or fat for frying	oil or fat for frying

Sift the flour and salt into a large mixing bowl. Gradually beat in the eggs and liquid to give a smooth batter. Leave in a cool place for about 30 minutes. Stir in the butter or oil just before cooking.

Put 5–10 ml./1–2 teaspoons of oil or a small knob of fat in a frying pan and heat thoroughly. Pour enough batter into the pan to give a paper-thin layer. Cook quickly for 1 to 2 minutes until lightly browned on the underside, then turn and cook on the other side. Remove from the pan, roll up, place on a warm plate and keep warm. Cook all the pancakes in the same way. Serve with sugar and lemon juice, jam or honey. *Serves 4*

Lemon soufflé

METRIC/IMPERIAL	AMERICAN
finely grated rind of 2 lemons	finely grated rind of 2 lemons
60 ml./4 tablespoons lemon juice	4 tablespoons lemon juice
3 eggs, separated	3 eggs, separated
100–175 g./4–6 oz. caster sugar	½–¾ cup superfine sugar
12 ml./¾ tablespoon powdered gelatine	¾ tablespoon powdered gelatin
60 ml./4 tablespoons water	4 tablespoons water
300 ml./½ pint double cream, stiffly whipped	1¼ cups heavy cream, stiffly whipped
small ratafia biscuits to decorate	small ratafia cookies to decorate

First prepare a 15 cm./6 in. soufflé dish. Cut a piece of greaseproof (waxed) paper three times the depth of the dish. Fold the paper in half to give a double thickness and tie it round the dish. Brush with melted butter the part that stands above the dish. Put the lemon rind, juice, egg yolks and sugar in a heatproof mixing bowl and place it over a pan of very hot water. Whisk until thick and creamy. Soften the gelatine in the cold water, add to the mixture and stir over heat until the gelatine has dissolved. Cool the mixture until it starts to stiffen, then fold in the cream. Whisk the egg whites until stiff, but not too dry, and fold them into the mixture. Spoon it into the prepared soufflé dish.

Leave the soufflé to set, then carefully remove the paper. Crush some of the biscuits (cookies) and press the crumbs round the sides. Decorate the top with the remaining biscuits (cookies). *Serves 5 to 6*

Above : Brandy soufflé ; Opposite top : Fruit salad ; Opposite bottom : Grape meringue flan

Brandy soufflé

METRIC/IMPERIAL	AMERICAN
about 12 sponge finger biscuits	about 12 sponge finger cookies
90 ml./6 tablespoons brandy or Curaçao	6 tablespoons brandy or Curaçao
100 g./4 oz. glacé cherries or mixed candied fruits, chopped	¾ cup chopped candied cherries or mixed candied fruits
25 g./1 oz. butter	2 tablespoons butter
25 g./1 oz. flour	¼ cup flour
150 ml./¼ pint milk	⅝ cup milk
150 ml./¼ pint single cream	⅝ cup light cream
50 g./2 oz. caster sugar	¼ cup superfine sugar
3 egg yolks	3 egg yolks
4 egg whites	4 egg whites

Arrange the sponge fingers in the bottom of a soufflé dish and add 45 ml./3 tablespoons brandy (or Curaçao) and the cherries or fruit. Melt the butter in a large pan. Stir in the flour and cook gently for 2 minutes. Gradually stir in the milk and cream. Bring slowly to the boil, stirring constantly, and cook until thickened. Add the sugar, the remaining brandy (or Curaçao) and the egg yolks. Fold in the stiffly beaten egg whites. Pile the mixture over the sponge fingers. Bake for 40 minutes in the centre of the oven preheated to moderate (180°C/350°F or Gas Mark 4). Serve at once.   *Serves 4 to 6*

Grape meringue flan

METRIC/IMPERIAL	AMERICAN
50 g./2 oz. butter	¼ cup butter
75 g./3 oz. dark brown sugar	⅜ cup dark brown sugar
75 g./3 oz. Demerara sugar	⅜ cup light brown sugar
120 ml./8 tablespoons golden syrup	8 tablespoons light corn syrup
225 g./8 oz. bran buds	8 oz. bran buds
small meringues to decorate	small meringues to decorate

For the filling

60 ml./4 tablespoons apricot jam, sieved	4 tablespoons apricot jam, sieved
45 ml./3 tablespoons water	3 tablespoons water
225 g./8 oz. white grapes, halved and pips removed	8 oz. white grapes, halved and seeds removed
50–75 g./2–3 oz. black grapes, halved and pips removed	2–3 oz. black grapes, halved and seeds removed

Melt the butter, the sugars and syrup in a large pan and stir to mix. Remove from the heat and stir in the bran buds. Press the mixture into a 10 cm./8 in. flan ring. Leave in a cool place for 2 to 3 hours to harden.

Heat the jam and water in a pan to make a glaze. Arrange the grapes in the flan case and brush with the warm glaze. When the glaze has cooled, arrange the small meringues round the edge. Serve with cream.

To vary, use crushed biscuits (cookies) or cornflakes instead of bran buds.   *Serves 4 to 6*

Fruit salad

Take a selection of dried fruits, such as dates, raisins, prunes and blanched nuts. Chop them and soak them in sherry for several hours until they are plump.

Then prepare for eating a selection of fresh fruits, such as oranges, apricots, grapes, apples, pears, bananas and plums. Slice apples, pears and bananas and sprinkle them with lemon juice to prevent them browning.

Mix all the fruits together, leaving a few to decorate as in the picture. Add a little orange juice and some sugar. The mixture should not be too sweet but should be quite moist. Arrange the fruit in a bowl, cover with foil, and chill in the refrigerator for a few hours. Sprinkle with flaked chocolate.

Baking

Buns/biscuits/scones/cakes/pastries

Brioches

METRIC/IMPERIAL	AMERICAN
45 ml./3 tablespoons water	3 tablespoons water
15 g./½ oz. dried yeast	½ oz. dried yeast
17.5 ml./1 tablespoon plus ½ teaspoon caster sugar	1 tablespoon plus ½ teaspoon superfine sugar
225 g./8 oz. flour	2 cups flour
2.5 ml./½ teaspoon salt	½ teaspoon salt
2 eggs, beaten	2 eggs, beaten
50 g./2 oz. butter, melted and cooled	¼ cup butter, melted and cooled

For the glaze

1 egg, beaten	1 egg, beaten
15 ml./1 tablespoon cold water	1 tablespoon cold water
pinch of sugar	pinch of sugar

Grease 12 8 cm./3 in. brioche tins or deep fluted patty (muffin) tins. Heat the water until lukewarm and pour into a small bowl. Whisk in the yeast and 2.5 ml./½ teaspoon of the caster (superfine) sugar. Leave in a warm place for about 10 minutes, or until frothy.

Sift the flour and salt into a warm bowl. Mix in the remaining sugar. Stir in the yeast mixture, eggs and butter. Beat by hand until the mixture leaves the sides of the bowl. Knead on a lightly floured board for 5 minutes. Place the dough in a slightly oiled plastic bag and leave to rise in a warm place until it has doubled in size – about 1½ hours.

Knead the dough well on a lightly floured board for about 5 minutes. Divide the dough into four equal pieces, then each piece into three. Use about three-quarters of each piece to form a ball. Place the balls of dough in the tins and firmly press a hole in the centre of each. Place the remaining small piece of dough in the hole. Place the tins on a baking sheet and cover with a large oiled plastic bag. Leave in a warm place to rise until light and puffy, about 1 hour.

Mix the ingredients for the glaze and brush it lightly on the buns. Bake in the oven preheated to very hot (230°C/450°F or Gas Mark 8) for about 10 minutes. Serve warm.

Makes 12

Right: Brioche
Opposite top: Doughnuts

136

Doughnuts

METRIC/IMPERIAL	AMERICAN
225 g./8 oz. flour	2 cups flour
pinch of salt	pinch of salt
25 g./1 oz. butter	2 tablespoons butter
25 g./1 oz. sugar	2 tablespoons sugar
1 egg, beaten	1 egg, beaten
150 ml./$\frac{1}{4}$ pint tepid milk	$\frac{5}{8}$ cup tepid milk
jam (optional)	jam (optional)
7 g./$\frac{1}{4}$ oz. fresh yeast, creamed with 5 ml./ 1 teaspoon sugar	$\frac{1}{4}$ oz. fresh yeast, creamed with 1 teaspoon sugar
deep fat for frying	deep fat for frying
caster sugar to sprinkle	superfine sugar to sprinkle

Sift the flour and salt together into a warm bowl. Rub in the butter, add the sugar and make a well in the centre. Add the egg and tepid milk to the creamed yeast and put the mixture into the well in the flour. Mix and beat well until smooth. Cover with a cloth and put in a warm place to rise until doubled in bulk, about 30 to 45 minutes.

Knead the dough well, then turn it on to a floured board. To make doughnut rings, roll out the dough and cut out rings. To make rounds, roll the dough into balls. Remember that it doubles in size when it rises.

To fill doughnuts with jam, make a small depression in the centre of each ball, put in a little jam and close the dough round the jam. Put the doughnuts on a greased baking sheet and leave in a warm place until they have doubled in size.

Fry in deep fat until golden brown, then roll in sugar.

Makes about 12

Hot cross buns

METRIC/IMPERIAL	AMERICAN
15 g./½ oz. fresh yeast	½ oz. fresh yeast
75 g./3 oz. sugar	⅜ cup sugar
just under 300 ml./½ pint tepid milk or milk and water	generous 1 cup milk or tepid milk and water
450 g./1 lb. flour	4 cups flour
pinch of salt	pinch of salt
2.5 ml./½ teaspoon ground allspice	½ teaspoon ground allspice
2.5 ml./½ teaspoon ground cinnamon	½ teaspoon ground cinnamon
50 g./2 oz. butter or margarine	¼ cup butter or margarine
75 g./3 oz. dried fruit	½ cup dried fruit
For the glaze	**For the glaze**
50 g./2 oz. sugar	¼ cup sugar
30 ml./2 tablespoons water	2 tablespoons water

Cream the yeast with 5 ml./1 teaspoon of the sugar. Add the milk, or milk and water, with a sprinkling of flour. Put in a warm place for 15 to 20 minutes, or until the surface is covered with bubbles.

Meanwhile sift the flour, salt and spices together in a warm bowl. Rub in the butter or margarine, then add the remaining sugar, the dried fruit and lastly the yeast mixture. Knead lightly but well. Cover the dough with a cloth and leave in a warm place to rise. This takes at least 1 hour.

Knead again, then cut the dough into 12 to 16 pieces and form them into rounds. Place them on warmed, lightly greased baking sheets, mark a cross on each bun with a knife and leave to rise for about 15 minutes.

Bake for about 12 minutes above the centre of the oven preheated to hot (220°C/425°F or Gas Mark 7). Mix the sugar and water for the glaze and brush the buns with it as soon as they come out of the oven.   *Makes 12 to 16*

Note: to make more prominent crosses, pipe on a cross of thick batter before baking.

Danish pastries

METRIC/IMPERIAL	AMERICAN
22 g./¾ oz. fresh yeast	¾ oz. fresh yeast
50 g./2 oz. sugar	¼ cup sugar
300 ml./½ pint tepid milk, or milk and water	1¼ cups tepid milk, or milk and water
450 g./1 lb. flour	4 cups flour
225 g./8 oz. butter	1 cup butter
1 egg, beaten	1 egg, beaten
For the filling	**For the filling**
jam, honey, marmalade or thick apple purée	jam, honey, marmalade or thick apple purée
For the icing	**For the frosting**
225 g./8 oz. icing sugar, sifted	1⅓ cups confectioners' sugar, sifted
little water	little water
glacé cherries and/or chopped nuts to decorate	candied cherries and/or chopped nuts to decorate

Cream the yeast with 5 ml./1 teaspoon of the sugar. Add the tepid liquid and a sprinkling of flour. Leave in a warm place for 15 to 20 minutes, or until the surface is covered with bubbles.

Sift the rest of the flour into a warm bowl. Rub in 50 g./2 oz. (¼ cup) of the butter, then add the rest of the sugar. Divide the remaining butter into two portions and leave them at room temperature to soften.

Add the yeast liquid to the flour, then stir in the egg. Mix well. Turn the dough on to a floured board and knead until smooth. Then put it back in the mixing bowl, cover with a cloth and leave to rise for about 1 hour, or until double its original size.

Knead the dough again and roll it out to an oblong shape, about 12 mm./½ in. thick. Spread it with half the softened butter. Fold in three, turn at right angles, then roll out once more. Then spread with the remaining butter and fold in three. Turn at right angles, roll again, then fold and turn. The dough is now ready to use and can be made into different shapes.

One of the most popular shapes is the envelope. Roll out the dough until it is about 6 mm./¼ in. thick. Cut into 10 cm./4 in. squares. Put a little of the chosen filling in the centre of

Viennese orange shortbreads

each square. Fold so that the corners of the square come to the centre, covering the filling.

Put the pastries on warmed greased baking sheets. Leave in a warm place for 20 minutes to rise. Bake for about 12 minutes above the centre of the oven preheated to hot (220°C/425°F or Gas Mark 7), then leave to cool.

Mix the icing (confectioners') sugar with enough water to give a thin coating. Spread the icing (frosting) over each pastry. Top with cherries and/or chopped nuts.

Makes about 12 pastries

METRIC/IMPERIAL	AMERICAN
100 g./4 oz. flour	1 cup flour
100 g./4 oz. cornflour	1 cup cornstarch
175 g./6 oz. butter	¾ cup butter
100 g./4 oz. icing sugar, sifted	⅔ cup confectioners' sugar, sifted
finely grated rind of 1 large orange	finely grated rind of 1 large orange
extra icing sugar to decorate	extra confectioners' sugar to decorate
For the filling	**For the filling**
finely grated rind of 1 large orange	finely grated rind of 1 large orange
75 g./3 oz. butter	⅜ cup butter
175 g./6 oz. icing sugar, sifted	1 cup confectioners' sugar, sifted

Sift the flour and cornflour (cornstarch) together into a bowl. Cream the butter, icing (confectioners') sugar and orange rind in a large mixing bowl until very soft and light. Gradually beat in the sifted flour and cornflour (cornstarch). Put the mixture into a piping bag with a 6 mm./½ in. rose nozzle and pipe out 14 to 16 neat roses on an ungreased baking sheet. Bake in the centre of the oven preheated to moderate (180°C/350°F or Gas Mark 4) for 15 to 20 minutes. The shortbreads should crisp without becoming too brown. Leave to cool on the baking sheet.

To make the filling, cream the orange rind, butter and icing (confectioners') sugar together. Sandwich the shortbreads with the filling and sprinkle the tops with a little extra icing (confectioners') sugar. *Makes 7 to 8*

Opposite : Hot cross buns and Danish pastries
Above : Viennese orange shortbreads

Date crunchies

METRIC/IMPERIAL	AMERICAN
100 g./4 oz. wholewheat flour	1 cup wholewheat flour
175 g./6 oz. rolled oats	1½ cups rolled oats
225 g./8 oz. butter or margarine	1 cup butter or margarine
225 g./8 oz. stoned dates	8 oz. pitted dates
30 ml./2 tablespoons water	2 tablespoons water
15 ml./1 tablespoon lemon juice	1 tablespoon lemon juice
15 ml./1 tablespoon clear honey	1 tablespoon clear honey
pinch of ground cinnamon	pinch of ground cinnamon

Place the flour and oats in a mixing bowl. Rub in the butter or margarine. Divide the mixture in two and press half over the bottom of a greased 18 cm./7 in. square tin.

Simmer the dates with the water until soft. Cool and stir in the lemon juice, honey and cinnamon. Spread the date mixture over the oat mixture in the tin and cover with the remaining oat mixture. Spread smooth. Bake in the oven preheated to moderate (180°C/350°F or Gas Mark 4) for 25 minutes. Cut into fingers while still warm. Cool in the tin and remove carefully. *Makes 14*

Flapjacks

METRIC/IMPERIAL	AMERICAN
100 g./4 oz. butter or margarine	½ cup butter or margarine
15 ml./1 tablespoon light brown sugar	1 tablespoon light brown sugar
60 ml./4 tablespoons golden syrup	4 tablespoons light corn syrup
225 g./8 oz. rolled oats	2 cups rolled oats
pinch of salt	pinch of salt

Melt the butter or margarine with sugar and syrup in a pan. Add the oats and salt and mix well. Spread the mixture smoothly in a 20 × 30 cm./8 × 12 in. tin and bake in the oven preheated to moderate (180°C/350°F or Gas Mark 4) for 15 to 20 minutes, or until golden brown and firm to the touch.

Cut into squares or fingers while warm. Cool in the tin and remove carefully. *Makes 18 to 24*

*Opposite top : Flapjacks
and Date crunchies
Opposite bottom : Popovers
Right : Scones*

Scones

METRIC/IMPERIAL
225 g./8 oz. flour
2.5 ml./½ teaspoon salt
5 ml./1 teaspoon
    bicarbonate of soda
10 ml./2 teaspoons cream of
    tartar
40 g./1½ oz. butter or
    margarine
about 150 ml./¼ pint milk

AMERICAN
2 cups flour
½ teaspoon salt
1 teaspoon baking soda
2 teaspoons cream of
    tartar
3 tablespoons butter or
    margarine
about ⅝ cup milk

Sift the flour, salt, soda and cream of tartar into a bowl. Cut the butter or margarine into small pieces and rub it into the flour until the mixture resembles fine breadcrumbs. Bind with enough milk to give a soft, but not wet, dough.

Roll out the dough on a floured board to 12 mm./½ in. thick. Cut with biscuit (cookie) cutters into 5 cm./2 in. rounds. Place the scones on a greased baking sheet and bake in the oven preheated to hot (220°C/425°F or Gas Mark 7) for 10 minutes, or until well risen and golden brown. Serve warm with butter and jam. *Makes about 12*
To vary, use half white flour and half wholemeal flour.

Popovers

METRIC/IMPERIAL
100 g./4 oz. self-raising
    flour
pinch of salt
2 eggs, beaten
225 ml./8 fl. oz. milk
10 ml./2 teaspoons oil or
    melted butter

AMERICAN
1 cup self-rising flour
pinch of salt
2 eggs, beaten
1 cup milk
2 teaspoons oil or melted
    butter

Sift the flour and salt into a large bowl. Beat in the eggs, then gradually whisk in the milk to make a smooth batter. Mix in the oil or melted butter just before cooking.

Half fill greased patty or popover tins with the batter and bake in the oven preheated to hot (220°C/425°F or Gas Mark 7) for 20 minutes. Then lower the temperature to moderate (180°C/350°F or Gas Mark 4) and bake for another 15 to 20 minutes, or until crisp and brown. Serve immediately with butter and jam or syrup, or with savoury toppings.
Makes 8 to 12

Scotch pancakes

METRIC/IMPERIAL	AMERICAN
100 g./4 oz. self-raising flour	1 cup self-rising flour
pinch of salt	pinch of salt
1 egg, beaten	1 egg, beaten
150 ml./¼ pint milk	⅝ cup milk

Sift the flour and salt into a large bowl. Beat in the egg, then gradually whisk in the milk to make a smooth batter.

Cook the pancakes on a lightly greased griddle, solid hot-plate or in a heavy frying pan. Heat the griddle, hotplate or frying pan and drop spoonfuls of the batter on to it. Cook for 1 to 2 minutes or until the top surface is covered in bubbles. Then turn with a palette knife and cook for the same time on the other side. To test if cooked, press gently with the edge of a knife – if no batter oozes out, they are cooked.

Serve warm or cold with butter and jam, or serve warm with savoury foods such as bacon or sausages. *Makes 10 to 12*

Rich dark chocolate cake

METRIC/IMPERIAL	AMERICAN
300 g./11 oz. caster sugar	1⅝ cups superfine sugar
90 ml./6 tablespoons water	6 tablespoons water
75 g./3 oz. cocoa powder	¾ cup cocoa powder
175 ml./6 fl. oz. milk	¾ cup milk
225 g./8 oz. butter	1 cup butter
4 eggs, separated	4 eggs, separated
225 g./8 oz. self-raising flour	2 cups self-rising flour
10 ml./2 teaspoons baking powder	2 teaspoons baking powder
150 ml./¼ pint double cream	⅝ cup heavy cream
150 ml./¼ pint single cream	⅝ cup light cream
icing sugar to decorate	confectioners' sugar to decorate

Put 75 g./3 oz. (⅜ cup) of the sugar in a pan with the water and cocoa and mix to a thick paste. Cook gently until the mixture is thick and shiny. Stir in the milk and leave to cool.

Cream the butter with the remaining sugar until the mixture is pale and fluffy. Beat in the egg yolks with the chocolate mixture. Sift together the flour and baking powder and fold into the mixture. Whisk the egg whites until stiff, then fold into the mixture. Divide the mixture between two sandwich (layer) cake tins, each about 20 cm./8 in. in diameter and 5 cm./2 in. deep, which have been lined with greased grease-proof (waxed) paper. Bake in the oven preheated to moderate (180°C/350°F or Gas Mark 4) for about 40 minutes or until the cake springs back when lightly pressed with a fingertip. Turn the cakes out, peel off the paper and cool on a rack.

Whisk the two types of cream together until thick. Split each cake in two across and use the cream to sandwich the layers together. Sprinkle with a little icing (confectioners') sugar.

Left : Scotch pancakes
Opposite : Rich dark chocolate cake

Christmas cake

METRIC/IMPERIAL	AMERICAN
2 eggs, beaten	2 eggs, beaten
175 g./6 oz. soft brown sugar	1 cup soft brown sugar
150 ml./¼ pint corn oil	⅝ cup corn oil
275 g./10 oz. flour	2½ cups flour
7.5 ml./1½ teaspoons baking powder	1½ teaspoons baking powder
pinch of salt	pinch of salt
45 ml./3 tablespoons sweet sherry or port	3 tablespoons sweet sherry or port
625 g./1 lb. 6 oz. mixed dried fruit	3⅔ cups mixed dried fruit
100 g./4 oz. mixed candied peel	⅔ cup mixed candied peel
75 g./3 oz. blanched, chopped almonds	¾ cup blanched, chopped almonds
45 ml./3 tablespoons glacé cherries, chopped	3 tablespoons chopped candied cherries

For the almond paste

METRIC/IMPERIAL	AMERICAN
350 g./12 oz. ground almonds	1½ cups ground almonds
175 g./6 oz. icing sugar, sifted	1 cup confectioners' sugar, sifted
1 egg, beaten	1 egg, beaten
1.25 ml./¼ teaspoon almond essence	¼ teaspoon almond extract
1.25 ml./¼ teaspoon vanilla essence	¼ teaspoon vanilla extract
little lemon juice	little lemon juice
apricot jam, melted and sieved	apricot jam, melted and sieved

For the royal icing

METRIC/IMPERIAL	AMERICAN
3 egg whites	3 egg whites
675 g./1½ lb. icing sugar, sifted	4 cups confectioners' sugar, sifted
10 ml./2 teaspoons fresh lemon juice	2 teaspoons fresh lemon juice
5 ml./1 teaspoon glycerine	1 teaspoon glycerine

Grease a 20 cm./8 in. round or 18 cm./7 in. square cake tin and line the bottom and sides with greased greaseproof (waxed) paper.

Beat together the eggs, brown sugar and oil. Sift the flour with the baking powder and salt and stir it into the egg mixture. Add the sherry or port. Fold in the fruit, peel, almonds and cherries. Put the mixture in the prepared tin and level the top with a knife.

Bake in the centre of the oven preheated to cool (150°C/300°F or Gas Mark 2) for 2½ to 3 hours, or until a skewer inserted in the centre comes out clean. Leave in the tin for at least 15 minutes before turning out on to a rack to cool.

When the cake is completely cold, wrap it in foil and leave it for at least a week to mature before covering with almond paste.

To make the almond paste, place all the ingredients, except the apricot jam, in a bowl and mix well to form a stiff paste. Then knead it until smooth. Roll out one-third of the paste to a round large enough to cover the top of the cake. Brush the cake with the apricot jam and cover with almond paste. Trim the edges. Roll out the remaining almond paste into a long strip the length and width of the sides of the cake. Brush the sides with apricot jam and cover with almond paste. Seal the join. Allow the almond paste to dry for three to four days before icing.

To make the icing, whisk the egg whites until frothy. Add the icing (confectioners') sugar a little at a time, beating well until the icing stands up in peaks when the beater is lifted out of the bowl. Beat in the lemon juice and glycerine. Cover with a damp cloth to prevent the icing hardening.

Stand the cake on a board, securing it with a little icing, then cover the top and sides thickly with about three-quarters of the icing. For a snow effect, press the back of a teaspoon into the icing and lift up so that small peaks form.

If liked, smooth the middle of the cake with a palette knife dipped in hot water, then pipe a border of rosettes round the smooth portion. Repeat round the lower edge.

Decorate with ribbon and Christmas ornaments.

Cider crumble cake

METRIC/IMPERIAL	AMERICAN
500 g./1 lb. 2 oz. self-raising flour	4½ cups self-rising flour
pinch of salt	pinch of salt
100 g./4 oz. soft brown sugar	⅔ cup soft brown sugar
65 g./2½ oz. chopped stoned dates	½ cup chopped pitted dates
45 ml./3 tablespoons black treacle	3 tablespoons molasses
300 ml./½ pint cider	1¼ cups apple cider
2 eggs, beaten	2 eggs, beaten

For the topping

METRIC/IMPERIAL	AMERICAN
35 g./1½ oz. butter	3 tablespoons butter
35 g./1½ oz. flour	⅜ cup flour
35 g./1½ oz. caster sugar	3 tablespoons superfine sugar
35 g./1½ oz. chopped walnuts	3 tablespoons chopped walnuts
2.5 ml./½ teaspoon ground cinnamon	½ teaspoon ground cinnamon
3 tablespoons plum jam	3 tablespoons plum jam

Grease a 13 cm./9 in. square tin. Line the base and sides with greased greaseproof (waxed) paper.

Sift the flour and salt into a bowl. Add the sugar and dates. Heat the treacle (molasses) and cider gently until the treacle (molasses) has dissolved. Stir the cider mixture and eggs into the flour and mix well. Put the mixture into the prepared tin and bake in the centre of the oven preheated to warm (170°C/325°F or Gas Mark 3) for 30 minutes.

To make the topping, rub together the butter, flour and sugar. Mix in the walnuts and cinnamon.

Remove the cake from the oven, spread it with jam and sprinkle with the nut topping. Return the cake to the oven for a further 20 minutes, or until a skewer inserted in the centre comes out clean. Leave the cake in the tin for 10 minutes, then turn it out on to a rack. When completely cold, wrap it in foil and keep for two days before cutting.

Opposite top : Christmas cake
Opposite bottom : Cider crumble cake

Family fruit cake

METRIC/IMPERIAL

225 g./8 oz. self-raising
   flour
pinch of salt
100 g./4 oz. lard, cooking
   fat or margarine (or
   mixture of fats)
90 g./3½ oz. caster sugar
175 g./6 oz. mixed dried
   fruit
5 ml./1 teaspoon finely
   grated orange rind
1 egg, beaten
about 100 ml./4 fl. oz. cold
   milk to mix

AMERICAN

2 cups self-rising flour
pinch of salt
½ cup lard, shortening or
   margarine (or mixture of
   fats)
just under ½ cup superfine
   sugar
1 cup mixed dried fruit
1 teaspoon finely grated
   orange rind
1 egg, beaten
about ½ cup cold milk to
   mix

Grease a 450 g./1 lb. loaf tin or a 15 cm./6 in. round cake tin.
Line the bottom and sides with greased greaseproof (waxed)
paper.

Sift the flour and salt into a bowl. Cut in the fat, then rub
it in finely with the fingertips. Add the sugar, fruit and orange
rind. Toss the ingredients lightly together. Using a fork, mix
to a semi-stiff batter with the egg and milk, stirring briskly
without beating. When evenly mixed, put the mixture in the
prepared tin.

Bake just above the centre of the oven preheated to
moderate (180°C/350°F or Gas Mark 4) for 1 to 1¼ hours or
until well risen and golden, or until a skewer inserted into the
centre comes out clean. Leave in the pan for 20 minutes, then
turn out on to a rack. Peel away the paper.

Ginger tea loaf

METRIC/IMPERIAL

275 g./10 oz. self-raising
   flour
10 ml./2 teaspoons ground
   ginger
2.5 ml./½ teaspoon ground
   mixed spice
100 g./4 oz. soft brown
   sugar
50 g./2 oz. lard or cooking
   fat
75 g./3 oz. golden syrup
75 g./3 oz. black treacle
1 large egg, beaten
90 ml./6 tablespoons milk

AMERICAN

2½ cups self-rising flour
2 teaspoons ground ginger
½ teaspoon ground mixed
   spice
⅔ cup soft brown sugar
¼ cup lard or shortening
⅜ cup light corn syrup
⅜ cup molasses
1 large egg, beaten
6 tablespoons milk

Grease a 1 kg./2 lb. (4 cup capacity) loaf tin. Line with greaseproof (waxed) paper, then brush with melted fat.

Sift the flour, ginger and spice into a bowl. Add the sugar
and toss lightly together. Melt the lard or cooking fat
(shortening), syrup and treacle (molasses) over low heat. Add
to the dry ingredients with the egg and milk, stirring briskly.
When the mixture is smooth, pour it into the prepared tin.

Bake in the centre of the oven preheated to warm (170°C/
325°F or Gas Mark 3) for 1¼ to 1½ hours, or until well risen
and firm, or until a skewer inserted in the centre comes out
clean. Leave in the tin for 5 minutes, then cool on a rack.

Opposite : Family fruit cake
Right : Ginger tea loaf
Below right : French chocolate squares

French chocolate squares

METRIC/IMPERIAL	AMERICAN
225 g./8 oz. plain chocolate	8 oz. (8 squares) semi-sweet chocolate
450 g./1 lb. sweet plain biscuits, crushed	1 lb. sugar cookies, crushed
75 g./3 oz. caster sugar	⅜ cup superfine sugar
100 g./4 oz. chopped walnuts	1 cup chopped walnuts
50 g./2 oz. butter	¼ cup butter
15 ml./1 tablespoon rum, brandy or strong coffee	1 tablespoon rum, brandy or strong coffee
1 small can (about 175 ml./ 6 fl. oz.) evaporated milk	1 small can (about ¾ cup) evaporated milk
2 eggs, beaten	2 eggs, beaten
For the fudge icing	**For the fudge frosting**
50 g./2 oz. plain chocolate	2 oz. (2 squares) semi-sweet chocolate
25 g./1 oz. butter	2 tablespoons butter
45 ml./3 tablespoons water	3 tablespoons water
175 g./6 oz. icing sugar	1 cup confectioners' sugar

Oil a 20 cm./8 in. shallow square cake tin. Line with foil, allowing it to extend about 2.5 cm./1 in. above the top edge of the tin. Brush with melted butter.

Break up the chocolate, put it in a heatproof bowl standing over a pan of hot water and leave until melted.

Put the crushed biscuits (cookies) in a bowl. Add the sugar and walnuts. Melt the butter, then stir in the rum, brandy or coffee and milk. Stir the mixture into the melted chocolate with the beaten eggs. Pour the mixture on to the biscuit (cookie) crumbs and stir thoroughly to combine. Transfer to the prepared pan and refrigerate overnight, or until firm and set.

Meanwhile make the fudge icing (frosting). Melt the chocolate and butter with the water in a heatproof bowl over a pan of hot water. Remove from the heat. Stir in the sifted icing (confectioners') sugar and beat until cool and thick.

Ease the cake out of the tin. Peel away the foil and cover the top with the fudge icing (frosting). When it has set, cut the cake into wedges. Keep any left-over cake in the refrigerator.

Makes 12 to 16

Lemon meringue pie

METRIC/IMPERIAL	AMERICAN
175 g./6 oz. quantity sweet shortcrust pastry dough	1½ cups quantity sweet shortcrust pastry dough
For the filling	**For the filling**
grated rind and juice of 2 lemons	grated rind and juice of 2 lemons
37 ml./2½ tablespoons cornflour	2½ tablespoons cornstarch
100–225 g./4–8 oz. caster sugar (see method)	½–1 cup superfine sugar (see method)
15–25 g./½–1 oz. butter	1–2 tablespoons butter
2 eggs, separated	2 eggs, separated

Roll out the dough and line a greased 20 cm./8 in. flan ring. Line with greased greaseproof (waxed) paper, fill with dry beans and bake in the oven preheated to fairly hot (200°C/400°F or Gas Mark 6) for about 15 minutes, or until the pastry is just set. Cool.

To make the filling, measure the lemon juice and make up to 300 ml./½ pint (1¼ cups) with cold water. Mix the cornflour (cornstarch) with the lemon juice and water and put in a pan with the grated rind and 50–100 g./2–4 oz. (¼–½ cup) sugar, according to taste. Add the butter and stir over gentle heat until the mixture has thickened. Remove from the heat and add the beaten egg yolks. Cook gently for several minutes. Taste and add more sugar if wished. Spoon the mixture into the pastry case.

Whisk the egg whites until very stiff, then gradually beat in 50g./2 oz. (¼ cup) of the remaining sugar. Fold the rest in slowly. For a softer meringue, gradually fold in all the sugar. If you want a firm meringue, use a mixer and gradually beat in all the sugar. Spoon the meringue over the lemon mixture so that it touches the pastry rim.

To serve freshly cooked : use the smaller quantity of sugar and brown for 20 minutes in the oven preheated to moderate (180°C/350°F or Gas Mark 4), or cook for 5 to 8 minutes in a hot oven (220°C/425°F or Gas Mark 7).

To serve cold : use the larger quantity of sugar and bake for at least 1 hour in the centre of the oven preheated to very cool (130°C/250°F or Gas Mark ½). *Serves 8*

Above : Lemon meringue pie
Opposite : Vanilla slices

Vanilla slices

METRIC/IMPERIAL	AMERICAN
225 g./8 oz. quantity puff pastry dough	2 cup quantity puff pastry dough
For the filling	**For the filling**
300 ml./½ pint double cream	1¼ cups heavy cream
sugar to taste	sugar to taste
few drops of vanilla essence	few drops of vanilla extract
red jam or jelly	red jam or jelly
little sifted icing sugar	little sifted confectioners' sugar

Roll out the dough on a floured board until paper thin. Cut into 15 or 18 fingers. Put the fingers of dough on greased baking sheets and leave in a cool place for about 30 minutes. Bake just above the centre of the oven preheated to very hot (240°C/475°F or Gas Mark 9) for about 10 minutes, or until risen and golden. Then lower the heat to warm (170°C/325°F or Gas Mark 3), or switch off, and cook for a further 5 minutes.

Allow the pastry to cool, then trim the edges with a sharp knife. Whip the cream until thick and add sugar to taste and a little vanilla essence (extract). Spread one-third of the slices with the cream. Top with another slice, then the jam or jelly and then a final pastry slice. Dust with icing (confectioners') sugar. *Makes 5 or 6*

Cream horns

METRIC/IMPERIAL

225 g./8 oz. quantity puff
    pastry dough
beaten egg for glaze
sugar for dredging
For the filling
strawberry jam
300 ml./½ pint double cream
5 ml./1 teaspoon vanilla
    essence
15 ml./1 tablespoon icing
    sugar, sifted
30 ml./2 tablespoons milk
strawberries to decorate
    (optional)

AMERICAN

2 cup quantity puff pastry
    dough
beaten egg for glaze
sugar for dredging
For the filling
strawberry jam
1¼ cups heavy cream
1 teaspoon vanilla extract
1 tablespoon confectioners'
    sugar, sifted
2 tablespoons milk
strawberries to decorate
    (optional)

Grease 12 cream horn tins. Rinse a large baking sheet with water and leave it damp.

Roll out the dough thinly and cut into 12 long strips, about 2.5 cm./1 in. wide. Brush one side of each strip with water. Wind each strip, with dampened side inside, round the tins, starting from the pointed end and overlapping the strip slightly so that there are no gaps. Place them on the baking sheet, brush with beaten egg and sprinkle with sugar. Leave in a cool place for 30 minutes.

Bake the horns just above the centre of the oven preheated to very hot (230°C/450°F or Gas Mark 8) for 20 to 25 minutes, or until golden brown and puffy. Gently lift each horn on to a rack to cool.

When the pastry is almost cold, carefully remove the tins. Put a little jam into the pointed end of each pastry horn. Whip the cream with the vanilla, icing (confectioners') sugar and milk until thick. Fill the horns. Decorate each one with a strawberry, if in season. *Makes 12*

Fruit tarts

METRIC/IMPERIAL

8 oz. quantity sweet
    shortcrust pastry dough
For the filling
selection of fruit such as
    pears, apples, grapes
lemon juice
175 g./6 oz. apricot jam
glacé cherries

AMERICAN

2 cup quantity sweet
    shortcrust pastry dough
For the filling
selection of fruit such as
    pears, apples, grapes
lemon juice
¾ cup apricot jam
candied cherries

Roll out the dough on a lightly floured board. Cut it into rounds and line 20 to 24 patty tins. Place small rounds of greased greaseproof (waxed) paper in the patty cases and fill each with some dry beans. Bake the cases in the oven preheated to fairly hot (200°C/400°F or Gas Mark 6) for about 20 minutes, or until cooked and golden. Cool on a rack.

Meanwhile, prepare the fruit. Peel, core and slice the pears thinly and dip each slice in lemon juice. Do the same with apples, but leave the peel on if it is red. Halve and seed the grapes.

Heat the apricot jam in a small pan with a few drops of lemon juice. Stir until blended, then sieve. Fill the cooked pastry cases with the prepared fruit and brush with the apricot glaze. Decorate with cherries. *Makes 20 to 24*

Above : Fruit tarts
Opposite : Cream horns

Apple strudel

METRIC/IMPERIAL	AMERICAN
175 g./6 oz. flour, preferably strong flour	1½ cups flour, preferably strong flour
pinch of salt	pinch of salt
15 ml./1 tablespoon oil	1 tablespoon oil
1 egg, beaten	1 egg, beaten
60 ml./4 tablespoons warm water	4 tablespoons warm water
melted butter to glaze	melted butter to glaze
icing sugar for dredging	confectioners' sugar for dredging
For the filling	**For the filling**
oil	oil
50 g./2 oz. fresh breadcrumbs	⅔ cup fresh breadcrumbs
50 g./2 oz. sultanas	⅓ cup golden raisins
½ kg./1 lb. cooking apples, peeled, cored and chopped	1 lb. cooking apples, peeled, cored and chopped
50 g./2 oz. sugar, or to taste	¼ cup sugar, or to taste
grated rind and juice of ½ lemon	grated rind and juice of ½ lemon
5 ml./1 teaspoon ground cinnamon	1 teaspoon ground cinnamon

Sift the flour and salt together into a bowl. Add the oil, egg and water to make a soft dough. Knead well until smooth. Leave covered for 30 minutes. Roll out half the dough at a time on a floured sheet of greaseproof (waxed) paper. Roll until paper thin. Brush with oil and sprinkle with breadcrumbs.

Mix the rest of the filling ingredients and spread half of the mixture on the dough to within 12 mm./½ in. of the edge. Wet the edges and roll up, using the greaseproof (waxed) paper to help. Seal the edges and place on a greased baking sheet. Brush with melted butter. Repeat the process with the rest of the dough and filling.

Bake in the oven preheated to hot (220°C/425°F or Gas Mark 7) for 40 minutes. Turn the oven down after 30 minutes if the pastry is getting too brown. Cut into pieces and sprinkle with sifted icing (confectioners') sugar.

Above : Apple strudel
Below : Mince pies
Opposite : Profiteroles

Mince pies

METRIC/IMPERIAL	AMERICAN
225 g./8 oz. quantity shortcrust pastry dough	2 cup quantity shortcrust pastry dough
450 g./1 lb. mincemeat	1 lb. mincemeat
beaten egg for glazing	beaten egg for glazing
icing sugar	confectioners' sugar

Lightly grease 12 deep bun tins (muffin pans).

Roll out the dough on a floured board and cut out 12 rounds to fit the bun tins (muffin pans). Line the bun tins (muffin pans) and fill with mincemeat. Moisten the edges of the dough with water. Cut out 12 smaller rounds for lids and place them on top of the pies. If wished, cut out a star in the centre of the lid. Pinch the edges of the dough together to seal. Brush the tops with beaten egg.

Bake just above the centre of the oven preheated to fairly hot (200°C/400°F or Gas Mark 6) for 20 minutes. Remove from the tins (pans) when just warm and sprinkle a little sifted icing (confectioners') over the top.   *Makes 12*

Profiteroles

METRIC/IMPERIAL
50 g./2 oz. butter
150 ml./¼ pint milk and
    water
65 g./2½ oz. flour, sifted
2 eggs, beaten
For the filling and icing
300 ml./½ pint double
    cream, lightly whipped
225 g./8 oz. icing sugar
15 ml./1 tablespoon cocoa
    powder
15 ml./1 tablespoon rum
15–30 ml./1–2 tablespoons
    warm water

AMERICAN
¼ cup butter
⅝ cup milk and water
good ½ cup flour, sifted
2 eggs, beaten
**For the filling and
frosting**
1¼ cups heavy cream,
    lightly whipped
1⅓ cups confectioners' sugar
1 tablespoon cocoa powder
1 tablespoon rum
1–2 tablespoons warm
    water

Put the butter, milk and water in a small pan and bring to the boil. Remove the pan from the heat. Add the flour all at once and beat the mixture until it forms a ball. Gradually beat in the eggs to make a smooth, shiny paste. Put the mixture in a large piping bag fitted with a 6 mm./½ in. plain nozzle. Pipe 20 blobs on to a greased baking sheet. Bake in the oven preheated to hot (220°C/425°F or Gas Mark 7) for 10 minutes, then reduce the temperature to fairly hot (190°C/375°F or Gas Mark 5) and cook for a further 15 to 20 minutes, or until golden brown.

Make a split with a sharp knife on one side of each bun to allow the steam to escape. Cool on a rack.

Fill each bun with whipped cream. Sift the icing (confectioners') with the cocoa into a bowl Stir in the rum and sufficient warm water to make a thick glacé icing. Spear each bun with a fork and dip the tops in the icing. Pile up in a pyramid as each one is finished. Serve the same day, as a dessert.

If you wish to serve the buns individually, ice the tops and keep the buns separate. *Makes 20 buns*

Drinks

Grenadine grape

METRIC/IMPERIAL
300 ml./$\frac{1}{2}$ pint grape juice
15 ml./1 tablespoon
  grenadine
1 egg white
crushed ice
soda water

AMERICAN
1$\frac{1}{4}$ cups grape juice
1 tablespoon grenadine
1 egg white
crushed ice
soda water

Thoroughly shake the grape juice, grenadine and egg white
with crushed ice. Strain into two glasses and fill with soda.

Serves 2

Above : Grenadine grape
Centre : Apple flame
Right : Whisky cola (left)
and Apricot cooler (right)

Apple flame

METRIC/IMPERIAL
225 ml./8 fl. oz. Calvados
  or apple brandy
30 ml./2 tablespoons
  Angostura bitters
1.2 l./2 pints boiling water
12 whole cloves
pared rind and juice of
  2 lemons
50 ml./2 fl. oz. Calvados to
  flame

AMERICAN
1 cup Calvados or applejack
2 tablespoons Angostura
  bitters
5 cups boiling water
12 whole cloves
pared rind and juice of
  2 lemons
$\frac{1}{4}$ cup Calvados to flame

Put the Calvados or apple brandy (applejack), bitters, boiling
water, cloves, lemon rind and juice in a pan over low heat.
Heat well. The mixture should not boil. Carefully pour extra
Calvados over the back of a spoon so that it floats on the
surface. Set alight and serve immediately. *Serves 10*

Whisky cola

METRIC/IMPERIAL
50 ml./2 fl. oz. Scotch
   whisky
15 ml./1 tablespoon
   Curaçao
15 ml./1 tablespoon lemon
   juice
2 dashes of Angostura
   bitters
crushed ice
cola
twist of orange rind to
   garnish

AMERICAN
¼ cup Scotch whisky
1 tablespoon Curaçao
1 tablespoon lemon juice
2 dashes of Angostura
   bitters
crushed ice
cola
twist of orange rind to
   garnish

Mix the whisky, Curaçao, lemon juice and Angostura bitters
in a glass. Add a heaped spoon of crushed ice and fill with
cola. Garnish with orange rind. *Serves 1*

Apricot cooler

METRIC/IMPERIAL
crushed ice
1 stewed or canned apricot
40 ml./1½ fl. oz. apricot
   brandy
15 ml./1 tablespoon lemon
   juice
5 ml./1 teaspoon icing
   sugar

AMERICAN
crushed ice
1 stewed or canned apricot
2½ tablespoons apricot
   brandy
1 tablespoon lemon juice
1 teaspoon confectioners'
   sugar

Pack a tumbler two-thirds full with crushed ice. Sieve the
apricot and mash well with a fork. Shake the apricot pulp
with the apricot brandy, lemon juice and sugar. Add ice to
shaker, shake again and pour, unstrained, into the glass.

Serves 1

Above : Glühwein ; Above right ; Peach froth ; Opposite left : Apple power ; Opposite right : Chocolate mint shake

Glühwein

METRIC/IMPERIAL	AMERICAN
3 bottles dry red wine	3 bottles dry red wine
½ bottle brandy	½ bottle brandy
300 ml./½ pint water	1¼ cups water
300 ml./½ pint orange juice	1¼ cups orange juice
juice of 2 lemons	juice of 2 lemons
thinly pared rind of	thinly pared rind of
1 lemon and 1 orange	1 lemon and 1 orange
6 cinnamon sticks	6 cinnamon sticks
1 orange stuck with 24	1 orange stuck with 24
cloves	cloves

Put all the ingredients in a large pan and simmer over low heat. Serve in mugs.   *Serves 20*

Peach froth

METRIC/IMPERIAL	AMERICAN
2 ripe peaches, peeled,	2 ripe peaches, peeled,
stoned and mashed	pitted and mashed
100 g./4 oz. sugar	½ cup sugar
350 ml./12 fl. oz. water	1½ cups water
350 ml./12 fl. oz. milk	1½ cups milk
10 ml./2 teaspoons clear	2 teaspoons clear honey
honey	2 egg whites
2 egg whites	grated nutmeg to garnish
grated nutmeg to garnish	

Simmer the peaches with the sugar and water for 45 minutes, then cool and strain. Put in a blender with the milk, honey and egg whites. Blend until frothy. Alternatively, whisk vigorously. Chill and serve sprinkled with nutmeg. *Serves 4*

Apple power

METRIC/IMPERIAL	AMERICAN
100 ml./4 fl. oz. apple brandy or Calvados	½ cup applejack or Calvados
300 ml./½ pint sweet cider	1¼ cups sweet apple cider
50 ml./2 fl. oz. Grand Marnier	¼ cup Grand Marnier
1.25 ml./¼ teaspoon ground cloves	¼ teaspoon ground cloves
1.25 ml./¼ teaspoon ground cinnamon	¼ teaspoon ground cinnamon
400 ml./¾ pint crushed ice	2 cups crushed ice

Mix all the ingredients in a blender and pour, unstrained, into tall glasses.

If you do not have a blender, shake very thoroughly, allow to stand for several minutes, then shake again before pouring, unstrained, into glasses. *Serves 4*

Chocolate mint shake

METRIC/IMPERIAL	AMERICAN
1.2 l./2 pints milk	5 cups milk
150 ml./½ pint ice cream	1¼ cups ice cream
100 ml./4 fl. oz. chocolate syrup	½ cup chocolate syrup
50 ml./2 fl. oz. peppermint syrup	¼ cup peppermint syrup
grated chocolate to decorate	grated chocolate to decorate

Put all the ingredients except the grated chocolate in a blender or shake thoroughly. Pour into glasses and decorate with chocolate. *Serves 6*

Above : White wine punch ; Centre : Pink pear ; Opposite : Fresh egg lemonade

White wine punch

METRIC/IMPERIAL
225 g./8 oz. cherries, stoned
450 g./1 lb. fresh
   pineapple cubes
100 ml./4 fl. oz. kirsch
50 g./2 oz. caster sugar
1 bottle dry white wine
6 dashes of Angostura
   bitters
600 ml./1 pint fresh or
   canned unsweetened
   pineapple juice
crushed ice

AMERICAN
8 oz. cherries, pitted
1 lb. fresh pineapple cubes
½ cup kirsch
¼ cup superfine sugar
1 bottle dry white wine
6 dashes of Angostura
   bitters
2½ cups fresh or canned
   unsweetened pineapple
   juice
crushed ice.

Marinate the cherries and pineapple in the kirsch and sugar overnight. Strain, reserving both the fruit and liquid.

Mix the wine, bitters, kirsch liquid and pineapple juice in a punch bowl or large jug. Add several handfuls of crushed ice and top with the reserved fruit. Serve in tall glasses about two-thirds full of punch mixture and fill up with soda.

Note: if fresh pineapple is unavailable, use canned fruit and omit the pineapple juice and sugar. *Serves 10 to 12*

158

Pink pear

METRIC/IMPERIAL	AMERICAN
1 pear, peeled, cored and sliced	1 pear, peeled, cored and sliced
thinly pared rind and juice of 1 lemon	thinly pared rind and juice of 1 lemon
50 g./2 oz. sugar	¼ cup sugar
225 ml./8 fl. oz. water	1 cup water
4 cloves	4 cloves
1 bottle rosé wine	1 bottle rosé wine
½ bottle port	½ bottle port
crushed ice	crushed ice
fresh pear slices to garnish	fresh pear slices to garnish
soda water	soda water

Put the pear slices, lemon rind, sugar, water and cloves in a pan. Simmer, covered, until the fruit is quite soft and pulpy. Remove the cloves and lemon rind. Allow to cool, then sieve the fruit with the juice.

Mix the wine, port and pear pulp with the juice of the lemon and several handfuls of crushed ice in a tall jug. Garnish with fresh pear slices and serve in glasses with soda to taste. *Serves 10 to 12*

Fresh egg lemonade

METRIC/IMPERIAL	AMERICAN
1 raw egg	1 raw egg
50 ml./2 fl. oz. lemon juice	¼ cup lemon juice
40 ml./1½ fl. oz. brandy	2½ tablespoons brandy
5 ml./1 teaspoon caster sugar	1 teaspoon superfine sugar
soda water	soda water
ice cube	ice cube

Blend or shake the egg, lemon juice, brandy and sugar. Strain into a tumbler and fill with chilled soda water. Top with an ice cube. *Serves 1*

Accompaniments to game

Fried crumbs

METRIC/IMPERIAL	AMERICAN
75 g./3 oz. fresh white breadcrumbs	1 cup fresh white breadcrumbs
50 g./2 oz. butter	¼ cup butter

Fry the crumbs in the hot butter until they are golden-brown. Drain on absorbent paper.

Game chips

Use about 700 g./1½ lb. potatoes to serve 4 to 6 people. Choose large potatoes, peel them and slice as thinly as possible. Soak the potato slices in water for about 1 hour, then drain them well and wrap in a clean cloth, keeping the slices separate so that they dry. Keep wrapped up for about 20 minutes, or until dry.

Fry the potato slices in deep hot fat until they are crisp and golden-brown. Drain on absorbent paper. Sprinkle with salt and serve.

Gravy

After roasting the meat, pour off all the fat from the roasting pan except for about 15 ml./1 tablespoon. Stir 15 ml./1 tablespoon flour into the fat and cook for a few minutes until it turns golden-brown. Gradually stir in 300 ml./½ pint (1¼ cups) stock, bring to the boil and cook until slightly thickened. Strain. If wished, a little gravy browning can be added to give colour and flavouring.

To make a thick gravy, use 30 l./2 tablespoons flour.

Pastry

Shortcrust pastry

METRIC/IMPERIAL	AMERICAN
225 g./8 oz. flour	2 cups flour
pinch of salt	pinch of salt
100 g./4 oz. butter, lard or cooking fat, or a mixture of fats	½ cup butter, lard or shortening, or a mixture of fats
45–60 ml./3–4 tablespoons water	3–4 tablespoons water

Sift the flour with the salt into a mixing bowl. Cut the fat into the flour with a knife, then rub it in with the fingertips. When the mixture resembles fine breadcrumbs, make a well in the centre and gradually add the water, mixing quickly with a knife. Add just enough water to give a firm dough.

Turn the dough on to a floured board and knead lightly until smooth. Wrap in greaseproof (waxed) paper or foil and chill in the refrigerator for 30 minutes before rolling out.

Note: To make a richer pastry, use 175 g./6 oz. butter only and add an egg yolk with the water, using slightly less water. Makes 225 g./8 oz. (2 cup) quantity dough.

Sweet shortcrust pastry

Add 15 ml./1 tablespoon caster (superfine) sugar to the flour and fat mixture.
Makes 225 g./8 oz. (2 cup) quantity dough.

Flaky pastry

METRIC/IMPERIAL	AMERICAN
225 g./8 oz. flour	2 cups flour
pinch of salt	pinch of salt
175 g./6 oz. butter, lard or cooking fat, or a mixture of fats	¾ cup butter, lard or shortening, or a mixture of fats
cold water to mix	cold water to mix

Sift the flour with the salt into a mixing bowl. Rub in about one-third of the fat, then mix in enough water to make an elastic dough. Roll out to an oblong on a lightly floured board.

Divide the remaining fat in two. If it is hard, soften it by pressing it with a knife. Cut one half of the fat into small pieces and put them on two-thirds of the oblong of dough. Fold the uncovered third of the dough over like an envelope, then fold the other third over that.

Turn the pastry at right angles, seal the ends of the dough, then press it at regular intervals with a lightly floured rolling pin. Then roll the dough into an oblong again and repeat the process with the remaining fat. Wrap the dough in greaseproof

(waxed) paper and chill for at least 30 minutes before rolling out.
Makes 225 g./8 oz. (2 cups) quantity dough.

Puff pastry

METRIC/IMPERIAL	AMERICAN
225 g./8 oz. flour	2 cups flour
pinch of salt	pinch of salt
225 g./8 oz. butter	1 cup butter
scant 150 ml./¼ pint ice-cold water	scant ⅝ cup ice-cold water
5 ml./1 teaspoon lemon juice	1 teaspoon lemon juice

Sift the flour with the salt into a mixing bowl. Rub in 25 g./1 oz. (2 tablespoons) of the butter and mix in the water and lemon juice. Turn the dough on to a lightly floured board and knead it for 2 to 3 minutes. Then roll it out to a square 12 to 18 mm./½ to ¾ in. thick.

Soften the remaining butter, if necessary, to make it pliable, and put it in the centre of the dough. Fold the dough over the butter like a parcel so that it is completely enclosed. Press the dough at regular intervals with a rolling pin to flatten it slightly. Then roll it out to a rectangle about 12 to 18 mm./½ to ¾ in. thick. Fold the dough in three, ends to middle, seal the edges and turn the pastry round once. Roll out again, fold and turn. Then wrap the pastry in greaseproof (waxed) paper or foil and chill for 15 minutes.

Repeat this process – fold, roll and turn twice, then chill – two more times. Then leave the dough in the refrigerator until it is required.
Makes 225 g./8 oz. (2 cup) quantity dough.

Salad dressings

French dressing

METRIC/IMPERIAL	AMERICAN
15 ml./1 tablespoon wine vinegar	1 tablespoon wine vinegar
salt and pepper	salt and pepper
1.25 ml./¼ teaspoon dry mustard	¼ teaspoon dry mustard
45 ml./3 tablespoons salad oil	3 tablespoons salad oil

Mix the vinegar with the seasoning and mustard, then whisk in the oil. Stir before using as the oil and vinegar separate on standing.

This quantity is enough for a large salad, serving 8 to 12 people. A larger quantity of dressing can be made and kept in a screw-top jar. Shake before using.

Vinaigrette dressing

METRIC/IMPERIAL	AMERICAN
30 ml./2 tablespoons wine or tarragon vinegar	2 tablespoons wine or tarragon vinegar
salt and pepper	salt and pepper
2.5 ml./½ teaspoon made mustard	½ teaspoon made mustard
15 ml./1 tablespoon salad oil	1 tablespoon salad oil
5 ml./1 teaspoon each of finely chopped gherkin, parsley and spring onion or shallot	1 teaspoon each of finely chopped dill pickle, parsley and scallion or shallot

Mix the vinegar with the seasoning and mustard, then whisk in the oil and stir in the other ingredients. Serve with asparagus, artichoke, avocado.

Soured cream dressing

METRIC/IMPERIAL	AMERICAN
60 ml./4 tablespoons soured cream	4 tablespoons sour cream
45 ml./3 tablespoons wine vinegar, or slightly less of lemon juice	3 tablespoons wine vinegar, or slightly less of lemon juice
salt and pepper	salt and pepper
about 15 ml./1 tablespoon sugar	about 1 tablespoon sugar

Mix all the ingredients together and adjust seasoning if necessary.
Makes 100 ml./4 fl. oz. (½ cup).

Sauces

Apple sauce

METRIC/IMPERIAL	AMERICAN
½ kg./1 lb. cooking apples, peeled, cored and sliced	1 lb. cooking apples, peeled, cored and sliced
50 g./2 oz. sugar	¼ cup sugar

Cook the apples in a pan with just enough water to stop them burning. Cook to a pulp, then sieve and add the sugar. Reheat and serve hot.

Béchamel sauce

METRIC/IMPERIAL	AMERICAN
400 ml./¾ pint milk	1⅞ cups milk
1 small onion, sliced	1 small onion, sliced
1 small carrot, sliced	1 small carrot, sliced
1 celery stalk, chopped	1 celery stalk, chopped
1 small bay leaf	1 small bay leaf
1 blade of mace	1 blade of mace
6 peppercorns	6 peppercorns
25 g./1 oz. butter	2 tablespoons butter
25 g./1 oz. flour	¼ cup flour
salt and pepper	salt and pepper

Put the milk in a pan with the vegetables, bay leaf, mace and peppercorns. Heat gently until it reaches boiling point. Then cover the pan, remove from the heat and leave to infuse for 20 minutes. Strain the milk.

Melt the butter in a pan, stir in the flour and cook over low heat for 2 minutes. Add the strained milk, stirring constantly. Season lightly. Bring to the boil and simmer for about 5 minutes, stirring constantly, until it thickens.
Makes 400 ml./¾ pint (1⅞ cups).

Bread sauce

METRIC/IMPERIAL	AMERICAN
1 onion, sliced	1 onion, sliced
4 cloves	4 cloves
300 ml./½ pint milk	1¼ cups milk
40 g./2 oz. fresh breadcrumbs	⅔ cup fresh breadcrumbs
25 g./1 oz. butter	2 tablespoons butter
salt and pepper	salt and pepper

Heat the onion, cloves and milk together for about 10 minutes, until the milk is well flavoured, then strain it. Return the milk to the pan, add the breadcrumbs and cook slowly, without boiling, until the crumbs become swollen. Add the butter in small pieces and season well.
Makes 300 ml./½ pint (1¼ cups).

Cheese sauce

METRIC/IMPERIAL	AMERICAN
25 g./1 oz. butter	2 tablespoons butter
25 g./1 oz. flour	¼ cup flour
300 ml./½ pint milk	1¼ cups milk
50 g./2 oz. Cheddar cheese, grated	½ cup grated Cheddar cheese
2.5 ml./½ teaspoon made mustard	½ teaspoon made mustard
salt and pepper	salt and pepper

Melt the butter in a pan, stir in the flour and cook for 2 minutes. Gradually stir in the milk and bring to the boil. Then lower the heat and simmer, stirring constantly, until the sauce has thickened. Stir in the cheese, mustard and seasoning and continue cooking over low heat until the cheese has melted.
Note: Gruyère, Emmenthal or Parmesan cheese may be used in place of Cheddar.
Makes 300 ml./½ pint (1¼ cups).

Cranberry sauce

METRIC/IMPERIAL	AMERICAN
225 g./8 oz. cranberries	8 oz. cranberries
300 ml./½ pint water	1¼ cups water
100 g./4 oz. sugar	½ cup sugar

Cook the cranberries in a pan with the water, crushing them with a spoon during cooking. When the cranberries are tender, sieve them. Add the sugar and stir until dissolved. Put in a dish to set if you want a jelly. For a hot sauce, add a little more water.
Note: If you prefer a thick sauce, do not sieve the cranberries.
Makes 400 ml./¾ pint (1⅞ cups).

Hollandaise sauce

METRIC/IMPERIAL	AMERICAN
3 egg yolks	3 egg yolks
salt and pepper	salt and pepper
30 ml./2 tablespoons lemon juice or white wine vinegar	2 tablespoons lemon juice or white wine vinegar
75 g./3 oz. butter	⅜ cup butter

Put the egg yolks, seasoning and lemon juice or vinegar into a large heatproof bowl over a pan of hot water, or in the top of a double boiler. Beat with a hand or electric whisk until the mixture is light and fluffy. When the mixture is thick, add a small piece of butter and whisk hard until it is well blended. Add the butter like this until it is all incorporated.
Serve hot or cold over vegetables, or with fish.   *Serves 6 to 7*

Mayonnaise

METRIC/IMPERIAL	AMERICAN
2 egg yolks	2 egg yolks
2.5 ml./½ teaspoon made English or French mustard	½ teaspoon made English or French mustard
1.25–2.5 ml./¼–½ teaspoon salt	¼–½ teaspoon salt
good shake of pepper	good shake of pepper
150 ml./¼ pint olive oil	⅝ cup olive oil
15–30 ml./1–2 tablespoons vinegar or lemon juice	1–2 tablespoons vinegar or lemon juice

Put the egg yolks and seasoning into a large bowl and beat well with a wooden spoon or whisk. Add the oil drop by drop, beating all the time. When all the oil has been incorporated, beat in vinegar or lemon juice to taste.

To make in a blender, put the yolks and seasoning in the container and switch on for a few seconds. Then add the vinegar or lemon juice (using the smaller amount) and blend. Then switch to a low speed and pour the oil in very steadily. Taste and add more vinegar or lemon juice if wanted. Then, still keeping the blender at low speed, add 15 ml./1 tablespoon boiling water.
Makes 150 ml./¼ pint (⅝ cup).

Tartare sauce

Make as for mayonnaise but add 15 ml./1 tablespoon chopped parsley, 10 ml./2 teaspoons chopped or whole capers and 10 ml./2 teaspoons chopped gherkins (dill pickle). Serve with fish.

Tomato sauce 1

METRIC/IMPERIAL	AMERICAN
1 kg./2 lb. ripe tomatoes, chopped	2 lb. ripe tomatoes, chopped
1 small onion, finely chopped	1 small onion, finely chopped
1 carrot, chopped	1 carrot, chopped
1 celery stalk, chopped	1 celery stalk, chopped
5 ml./1 teaspoon chopped parsley	1 teaspoon chopped parsley
salt and pepper	salt and pepper
pinch of sugar	pinch of sugar

Put the tomatoes in a pan with the vegetables. Add the parsley, salt, pepper and sugar. Simmer until the tomatoes have cooked almost to a purée. Sieve the mixture and adjust the seasoning if necessary.

If a thicker sauce is required, it can be returned to the pan and simmered until it is the right consistency.
Makes 300 ml./½ pint (1¼ cups).

Tomato sauce 2

METRIC/IMPERIAL	AMERICAN
30 ml./2 tablespoons olive oil	2 tablespoons olive oil
1 small onion, finely chopped	1 small onion, finely chopped
2 cans Italian tomatoes (about 675 g./1½ lb.)	2 cans Italian tomatoes (about 1½ lb.)
30 ml./2 tablespoons tomato purée	2 tablespoons tomato purée
10 ml./2 teaspoons chopped fresh basil, or 2.5 ml./½ teaspoon dried basil	2 teaspoons chopped fresh basil, or ½ teaspoon dried basil
5 ml./1 teaspoon sugar	1 teaspoon sugar
2.5 ml./½ teaspoon salt	½ teaspoon salt
freshly ground black pepper	freshly ground black pepper

Heat the oil in a pan. Add the onion and cook until it is soft but not coloured. Add the tomatoes, coarsely chopped but not drained, and all the other ingredients. Partly cover the pan and simmer over very low heat for about 40 minutes, stirring occasionally.

Sieve the sauce and adjust the seasoning if necessary.
Makes 300 ml./½ pint (1¼ cups).

Parsley sauce

METRIC/IMPERIAL	AMERICAN
25 g./1 oz. butter	2 tablespoons butter
25 g./1 oz. flour	¼ cup flour
300 ml./½ pint milk	1¼ cups milk
salt and pepper	salt and pepper
30 ml./2 tablespoons chopped parsley	2 tablespoons chopped parsley

Melt the butter in a pan, stir in the flour and cook for 2 minutes. Gradually stir in the milk and bring to the boil. Then simmer, stirring constantly, until the sauce thickens. Stir in the parsley just before serving.
Note: if the sauce is for fish, you may use half milk and half liquid from cooking the fish.
Makes 300 ml./½ pint (1¼ cups).

Lemon sauce

Make as for parsley sauce but add the grated rind of 1 lemon to the flour and 15 ml./1 tablespoon lemon juice to the thickened sauce.

Stocks

Brown stock

METRIC/IMPERIAL	AMERICAN
1½ kg./3 lb. beef bones	3 lb. beef bones
1 celery stalk, sliced	1 celery stalk, sliced
2 carrots, quartered	2 carrots, quartered
2 onions, quartered	2 onions, quartered
bouquet garni	bouquet garni
salt and pepper	salt and pepper
3 l./7 pints water	4½ quarts water

Put the bones in a very large pan and fry over gentle heat for about 15 minutes. Do not add any fat unless the bones are very dry. Add the vegetables and cook until lightly coloured, then add the herbs, seasoning and water. Bring slowly to the boil. Skim off scum occasionally. Then reduce the heat and simmer, half covered, for about 3 hours. Strain the stock and leave it to get cold. Then remove fat from the surface.
Makes about 2.2 l./4 pints (5 pints).

White stock

Make as for brown stock but use veal bones and do not brown them before adding water.

Chicken stock

METRIC/IMPERIAL	AMERICAN
chicken giblets, excluding the liver	chicken giblets, excluding the liver
1 onion, halved	1 onion, halved
little fat	little fat
1.1 l./2 pints water	5 cups water
salt and pepper	salt and pepper
bouquet garni	bouquet garni

Put the giblets and onion in a large pan with a small amount of fat. Cover and cook quickly until the ingredients are lightly coloured. Remove the pan from the heat and add the water, seasoning and bouquet garni. Simmer gently for 1 to 2 hours, or until the stock has a strong chicken flavour. Strain, cool and skim off the fat.

Note: a chicken carcass can also be included with the giblets. To make turkey, duck or game stock, use the giblets of the appropriate bird.

Makes about 600 ml./1 pint (2½ cups).

Consommé

METRIC/IMPERIAL	AMERICAN
½ kg./1 lb. shin of beef, cut into pieces	1 lb. shank of beef, cut into pieces
1.5 l./2½ pints brown stock	1 quart brown stock
1 bay leaf	1 bay leaf
salt and pepper	salt and pepper
2 egg whites plus shells	2 egg whites plus shells
sherry to taste	sherry to taste

Put the meat in a large pan with the stock and bring to the boil. Add the bay leaf and a little seasoning. Simmer steadily, covered, for about 1½ hours. Strain the consommé and return it to the pan. Add the egg whites and shells and simmer very gently for about 10 minutes. (The egg whites and shells clear the liquid.) Strain the consommé and add the sherry.

Makes about 1.1 l./2 pints (5 cups).

Fish stock

METRIC/IMPERIAL	AMERICAN
225 g./8 oz. fish heads, bones, skin and trimmings	8 oz. fish heads, bones, skin and trimmings
1 small onion	1 small onion
¼ bay leaf	¼ bay leaf
1 clove	1 clove
parsley sprig	parsley sprig

Put all the fish trimmings in a pan and cover with cold water. Add the remaining ingredients, bring to the boil, cover and simmer for 20 minutes. Strain.

Makes about 1.1 l./2 pints (5 cups).

Vegetable stock

METRIC/IMPERIAL	AMERICAN
15 g./½ oz. butter	1 tablespoon butter
½ kg./1 lb. carrots, quartered	1 lb. carrots, quartered
½ kg./1 lb. onions, quartered	1 lb. onions, quartered
4 celery stalks, sliced	4 celery stalks, sliced
2 l./3½ pints water	2 quarts water
5 ml./1 teaspoon tomato purée	1 teaspoon tomato purée
salt and pepper	salt and pepper

Melt the butter in a large pan. Add the vegetables and cook until lightly coloured. Then add the water, tomato purée and seasoning. Simmer for about 2 hours, or until the stock has a good flavour, then strain.

Makes about 1.5 l./2½ pints (1 quart).

Tomato purée

METRIC/IMPERIAL	AMERICAN
350 g./12 oz. ripe tomatoes, chopped	12 oz. ripe tomatoes, chopped
salt and pepper	salt and pepper
1 bay leaf	1 bay leaf
1 onion slice	1 onion slice
knob of butter	knob of butter

Put all the ingredients in a saucepan and simmer over very low heat until they form a thick pulp, about 10 to 15 minutes. Sieve the pulp and adjust the seasoning if necessary, adding a little sugar if there is any sharpness.

Makes about 300 ml./½ pint (1 cup).

Savoury butter pats

Savoury butter pats

Soften 50 g./2 oz. (¼ cup) butter in a bowl with a wooden spoon. Mix in the flavouring as required, then spread the butter to about 6 mm./¼ in. thick on greaseproof (waxed) paper and chill. Cut into small rounds. Serve with grilled (broiled) meat and fish.

Anchovy butter

Soak 4 anchovy fillets in milk, then mash them and add to the butter with a little black pepper and anchovy essence (extract).

Maître d'hôtel butter

Add to the butter 10 ml./2 teaspoons chopped parsley, a few drops of lemon juice and salt and pepper.

Parsley butter

Melt an extra 15 g./½ oz. (1 tablespoon) butter in a pan. When it is lightly browned, add 5 ml./1 teaspoon chopped parsley and a dash of Worcestershire sauce.

Garlic butter

Add crushed garlic to taste.

Index

Alaska, cherry grapefruit 118
Almonds, fried and carrots 33
Anchovy butter 165
Apple and carrot salad 24
    baked with orange 126
    Charlotte 124
    flame 154
    power 157
    sauce 161
    strudel 152
Apricot cooler 155
    fool 128
    nut stuffing 80
Artichoke hearts and aspara-
    gus 9
    vinaigrette 10
Asparagus on artichoke hearts 9
Aubergines (eggplants), stuffed
    29
Avocado cream dip 7
    surprise 6

Bamboo shoots and pork 76
Banana and lemon cream 127
Barbecue sauce 111
Barbecued beef saté 111
    chicken drumsticks 110
Beans and salami salad 8
    Boston baked 34
    green with tomatoes 118
    haricot with lamb 80
Béchamel sauce 161
Beef and prune stew 70
    and vegetable soup 15
    stew 73
    barbecued 111
    Bourguignonne 67
    braised whirls 72
    curry 73
    fillet, stuffed 71
    pepperpot 74
    risotto Milanaise 43
Berry mould 123
Bisque, crab 16
    lobster 19
Bordelaise kidneys 85
Bornholm omelet 36
Bortsch, speedy 118
Boston baked beans 34
Bourguignonne beef 67
Braised beef whirls 72
    liver 89
Brandy butter 132
    soufflé 134
Bread sauce 162
Brigade pudding 128
Brioches 136
Broccoli 116
    Polonaise 32
Brown stock 163
Burghul salad 26
Butter, brandy 132
    savoury 165

Cabbage, red 32
Cacciatore chicken 91
cakes 142–146
Canelloni 50
Caramel custard 126
Carpetbag steaks 68
Carrot and apple salad 24
    and fried almonds 33
    creamed 114
Casserole, cabbage and tomato
    107
    chick pea 108
    of duck 99
    rice and vegetable 106
    vegetable 107
Cassoulet 81
Cauliflower Niçoise 120
    salad 8
    soup 17
    surprise 104
    with brown sauce 35
Chablis halibut 59
Cheese and potato ring 34
    cold soufflé 40
    cream with avocado 6
    log 116
    omelet 38
    sauce 162
    soufflé 36
    with potato 29
Cheesecake, orange 124
    raspberry 131
Cherry grapefruit Alaska 118
Chick pea casserole 108
Chicken and pear vol-au-vent 93
    barbecued 110
    Cacciatore 91
    chowder 20
    cream soup 17
    curry 96
    drumsticks 110
    fried, Italienne 97
        with green peppers 94
    in red wine 95
    in wine, Italian style 92
    liver pâté 12
    peach salad 24
    pie, Old English 93
    pilau 42
    stock 164
    terrine 95
    with white wine and mush-
        rooms 90
Chinese soups 15–16
Chocolate cake, rich, dark 142
    mint shake 157
    squares, French 147
Christmas cake 144
    pudding 132
    iced 130
Cider crumble cake 144
Citrus fruit cocktail 120
    green salad 25
Consommé 164

Crab bisque 16
    with black beans 53
Cracked wheat salad 26
Cranberry sauce 162
Cream horns 151
Creamed carrots 114
    kidneys 85
    turkey Duchesse 99
Crêpes 133
Crisp-topped noodles 118
Crown roast 82
Curry, beef 73
    chicken 96

Danish pastries 138
Date crunchies 140
Dips 7
Doughnuts 137
Duchesse potatoes 114
    turkey 99
Duck casserole 99
    roast stuffed 97
        with Marsala 98
Dumplings, mustard 84

Egg au gratin 40
    lemonade 159
    scrambled 39
Escalopes of veal, Bolognese 65
    Milanaise 65
    Turin-style 66

Family fruit cake 146
Fennel, French fried 30
Figs, stuffed 124
Fillet of beef, stuffed 71
Fish, fried 56
    in a jacket 56
    stock 164
Flaky pastry 160
Flapjacks 140
Fool, apricot 128
Forcemeat stuffing 100
French chocolate squares 147
    dressing 161
Fricassée sweetbreads 84
    veal 66
Fried almonds with carrots 33
    chicken & peppers 94
        Italienne 97
    crumbs 160
    fish, mixed 56
Fruit cake 146
    meringue trifle 128
    salad 135
    tarts 151

Gammon (ham) with pineapple
    and corn sauce 78
Garbanzo casserole 108

Garlic bread 116
    butter 165
Gazpacho 20
Ginger tea loaf 146
Gingerbread 120
Glühwein 156
Gnocchi 51
Goose 101
Grape grenadine 154
    meringue flan 134
Grapefruit and kipper dip 7
Grenadine, grape drink 154

Haddock and mushroom
    scallops 59
    Charlotte 114
Halibut, Chablis 59
    with egg and lemon sauce 57
Ham, stuffed rolls 79
    sweet and sour 118
    with pineapple 78
Hare in Madeira sauce 102
    jugged, Landès-style 103
Haricot beans with lamb 80
Harlequin soufflé omelet 115
Hawaiian salad 23
Herring, Normandy 58
    orange salad 8
Hollandaise sauce 162
Hors d'oeuvre 8
Hot cross buns 138

Iced Christmas pudding 130
Icing, royal 144
Italian fried chicken 97
    -style chicken 92

Jugged hare 103

Kebabs 82, 86

Kidneys Bordelaise 85
    creamed 85
    kebabs 86
    lemon garlic 89
    with spring onions 87
Killarney hot-pot 75
Kipper and grapefruit dip 7

Lamb, cassoulet 81
    crown roast 82
    kebabs 82
    loin, with haricot beans 80
    roast with stuffing 80
Landès-style jugged hare 103
Lasagne 47
Leeks Mornay 28
Lemon and banana cream 127

garlic kidneys 89
meringue pie 148
soufflé 133
Lemonade, fresh egg 159
Lentil rissoles 108
Liver, braised with mush-
rooms and rice 89
Sicilienne 86
sauce with tagliatelle 49
with spring onions 88
Lobster bisque 19
Loin of lamb with beans 80
Lychees, and sweet and sour
pork 78

Macaroni, Mexican 49
Madeira sauce with hare 102
Madrilène peaches 114
Maître d'hôtel butter 165
Marsala with duck 98
Mayonnaise 162
green 112
Mediterranean stuffed tomatoes
28
Melon and Parma ham 9
and pineapple dip 7
balls with lemon sauce 11
hot with ginger 116
Meringue, fruit trifle 128
grape flan 134
lemon pie 148
Mexican macaroni 49
Mince pies 152
Minestrone 21
Mocha pots 123
Mornay, leeks 28
veal 63
Mussels marinière 55
Mustard dumplings 84

Neapolitan pizza 51
Niçoise, cauliflower 120
salad 8, 113
spinach 109
Noodle, crisp-topped 118
with meat sauce 44
Normandy herring 58
pork 77

Old English chicken pie 93
Omelet, Bornholm 36
cake 39
cheese 38
harlequin soufflé 115
soufflé 40
Orange and chicory salad 27
cheesecake 124
filling in baked apples 126
herring salad 8
sauce with duck 97
shortbread 139
water ice 127
Onion soup 18
Oxtail hotch-potch 84

Pancakes 133
Scotch 142
Parma ham with melon 8
Parsley butter 165
sauce 163
Pasta slaw 24
Pastry 160–161
Pâté, chicken liver 12
maison 12

speedy spiced 11
Peach, chicken salad 24
froth 156
madrilène 114
stuffed 11
Pear, and chicken vol-au-vent
93
pink (drink) 159
Peas and cucumber 33
Pepperpot beef 74
Peppers, red 32
sweet, with ham 76
Pheasant 100
Picnic 112–3
Pie, chicken 93
lemon meringue 148
mince 152
steak and kidney 69
Pineapple mousse 130
soufflé pudding 117
Pink pear 159
Pipérade 38
Pizza, Neapolitan 51
with olives and herbs 48
Pork and bamboo shoots 76
Normandy 77
sweet and sour 78
Popovers 141
Potato, Duchesse 114
salad 113
with cheese 29
Prawn and egg flower soup 16
and turbot salad 13
balls in sweet and sour sauce
54
in cream sauce 13
Profiteroles 153
Prunes and beef stew 70
Puff pastry 161
Punch, white wine 158

Raspberry cheesecake 131
Ratatouille 30
Red cabbage 32
peppers 32
Rice, fried, with ham and bean
sprouts 44
Risotto 43
beef, Milanaise 43
Rissoles, lentil 108
Roast, crown 82
duck 95, 98
goose 101
lamb with stuffing 80
pheasant 100
turkey with stuffing 100
Royal icing 144

Salad, American 22
bean and salami 8
burghul 26
cauliflower 8
citrus green 25
dressings 161
Hawaiian 23
mixed 22
mushroom, raw 8
rice 8
orange herring 8
Niçoise 8, 113
potato 113
summer 27
tomato and orange 25
winter 27
salami and bean 8
Salmon Walewska 60

sauces 161–163
Scallops, Breton-style 61
with peppers 60
Scones 141
Scotch pancakes 142
Scrambled eggs 39
Semolina gnocchi 51
Shortcrust pastry 160
Shortbread, Viennese orange
139
Shrimp and egg flower soup 16
balls 54
in cream sauce 13
Sicilienne liver 86
Sole, grilled 53, 120
Normande 52
Soufflé, brandy 134
cheese 36
cold cheese 40
harlequin omelet 115
omelet 40
pineapple 117
Soured cream dressing 161
Spaghetti Bolognese 46
with tomato and anchovy 45
and olives 47
Spinach Niçoise 109
Steak and kidney pie 69
carpetbag 68
upside-down pie 70
Stocks 163–164
Strudel, apple 152
vegetable 105
Stuffed aubergines (eggplants)
29
duck 97
figs 124
fillet of beef 71
French loaf 113
goose 101
ham rolls 79
lamb 80
tomatoes 28
turkey 100
Summer salad 27
soup, chilled 18
Sweet and sour ham 118
pork 78
Sweetbreads, fricassée 84
Swiss veal 62

Tagliatelle with liver sauce 49
Tartare sauce 163
Tarts, fruit 151
Terrine of chicken 95
Tomato and celery soup 19
and orange salad 25
frosted cocktail 10
juice cocktail 116
purée 164
stuffed 28
sauce 163
with green beans 118
Trifle, meringue fruit 128
Tripe, French-style 84
Trout, grilled (broiled) 54
Tuna fish, Provençale 58
with avocado 6
Turkey, creamed, Duchesse 99
roast, stuffed 100

Vanilla slices 148
Veal birds 64
escalope Bolognese 65
Milanese 65
Turin-style 66

fricassée 66
Mornay 63
Swiss 62
Vegetable and beef, Chinese
soup 15
and beef stew 73
and rice casserole 106
casserole 107
stock 164
strudel 105
Viennese orange shortbread 139
Vinaigrette, artichokes 10
dressing 161
Vol-au-vent, chicken and pear
93

Water ice 127
Whisky cola 155
white stock 164
wine punch 158
with chicken & mushrooms
90
Winter salad 27

Acknowledgments

The Publishers would like to thank the following people for their assistance in providing photographs and accessories for this book: American Rice Council: 42, 43; Bryce Attwell: 17, 28, 44, 96; John Searle Austin: 27; Barnaby Picture Library: 44, 45; Birds Eye: 19, 90; Barry Bullough: 14, 15; California Prune Advisory Bureau: 70; Canned and Packaged Foods Bureau: 135; Carrier Cookshops: 115, 116; Chiltonian Ltd.: 7; Cordon Bleu: 92; Crocks Reject China: 70, 71, 114, 115; Dutch Dairy Bureau: 37; Eden Vale Ltd.: 47; Egg Board: 38; Food from France (Sopexa): 94, 103; Fratelli Febbri Editore: 9, 50, 53; Fruit Producers' Council: 24, 79, 93, 125, 151; Melvin Grey: 31, 50, 122, 123, 130, 131, 143; Harvey Nichols: 19; Herring Industry Board: 58; Kellog Co. of Great Britain Ltd.: 135; Paul Kemp: 87, 88; Mike Leale: 52, 68, 72, 101, 110, 117, 119, 129, 130, 134; John Lee: 8, 10, 11, 13, 18, 23, 24, 28, 30, 34, 35, 36, 38, 39, 40, 41, 42, 53, 59, 61, 73, 75, 77, 78, 82, 83, 85, 86, 95, 97, 98, 99, 100, 101, 102, 107, 109, 125, 126, 127, 132, 133, 138, 139, 148, 149, 160, 162, 163, 164; Neil Lorimer: 76, 77; Mazola: 145, 152; David Mellor Ironmonger: 33, 74, 75, 128; National Dairy Council: 127; New Zealand Lamb Information Bureau: 80; Norman Nicholls: 10, 11, 12, 13, 26, 62, 71, 81, 89, 106, 108, 109, 122, 140, 154, 155, 156, 157, 158, 159; PAF International: 9, 17, 29, 32, 46, 47, 48, 56, 57, 61, 79, 94, 98, 124, 136, 137, 146, 147; Pasta Foods Ltd.; 24, 27; Pentangle Photography: 27; Roger Phillips: 2–3, 165; Photopad: 8, 49, 51, 54, 91; Potato Marketing Board: 29; RHM Foods Ltd.: 48, 93, 132, 140, 142; Rice Council: 89, 98; Syndication International: 12, 18, 23, 46, 55, 64, 65, 69, 74, 104, 112, 113, 126, 137, 150: Tabasco Sauce: 99; Taunton Cider: 145; Tupperware: 6, 27; Wedgwood from Gered: 16, 128; John West Foods Ltd.: 20, 58; White Fish Authority: 56; Wilson & Gill: 60, 63.